The
Woodwright's
Eclectic
Workshop

The Woodwright's Eclectic Workshop

Roy Underhill

The

University

of North

Carolina

Press

Chapel Hill

& London

The paper in this book meets the guidelines for

permanence and durability of the Committee on

Production Guidelines for Book Longevity of the

Council on Library Resources.

95 94 93 92 91

5   4   3   2   1

Library of Congress Cataloging-in-Publication Data

Underhill, Roy.

  The woodwright's eclectic workshop / by Roy Underhill.

    p.   cm.

  Includes index.

  ISBN 0-8078-2003-2 (cloth : alk. paper).—ISBN 0–8078–4347–4 (pbk. : alk. paper)

  1. Woodwork.   I. Title.

TT185.U52   1991

684'.08—dc20   91-24669

                CIP

Photo credits:

Colonial Williamsburg Foundation, pp. 104, 113, 116

Connecticut Historical Society, p. 56

Geary Morton, pp. 165, 169

Gunston Hall, p. 83

Lowie Museum of Anthropology, University of California at Berkeley, pp. 193, 194, 196

Mariner's Museum, Newport News, Va., pp. 185, 186

Rare Book Collection, UNC Library, Chapel Hill, N.C., p. 120

Tart Collection, p. 11 (bottom)

Valentine Museum, Heustis Cook Collection, Richmond, Va., pp. 29, 30, 32

Yale University Art Gallery, p. 82

U.S. Air Force, p. 160

All other photographs by R.E.U.

Parts of this book have previously appeared, in somewhat different form, in *WOOD Magazine* and in the National Historical Society publications *Architectural Treasures of America* and *The Modern Carpenter and Joiner and Cabinetmaker*.

Contents

About This Book

The Woodwright's Eclectic Workshop is the fourth in the series of books that I have written to accompany the PBS television series, "The Woodwright's Shop." The third book, *The Woodwright's Workbook*, was published in 1986. This book, then, contains projects, stories, and articles from the past five years in the Woodwright's Shop. Joining a half-decade of work into a single piece inevitably leads to some odd combinations that I hope you will find curious, amusing, useful, and informative. Think of this book as a chest packed full of tools, books, clothes, and a picnic lunch thrown in for good measure. You can't work all the time.

Over the past five years I have worked with a lot of folks, most of them right near home. I have an easier time than most people who do research on early trades. Here in Colonial Williamsburg, all I need to do to pick the brains of the world's leading authorities on many woodworking crafts is to simply walk down the street and ask. I say this not as a boast, but in acknowledgment of a great privilege.

The high standards of this community of craftsmen-scholars are due in large part to the stewardship of Earl L. Soles, Jr., longtime director of historic trades at Colonial Williamsburg. Contributors to this book from within the department of historic trades are almost too numerous to mention safely without leaving someone out, but here I go. First, in the building trades, thanks to Bill Weldon, Garland Wood, Russell Steele, Frank Grimsley, Dan Whitten, Robert Watson, and the late Dave Robinson. In the wheelwright's shop, thanks to Dan Stebbins, John Boag, and Ron Vinyard. In the blacksmith's shop, thanks to Pete Ross, Rick Guthrie, Ken Schwarz, and Jay Close. In the gunsmith's shop, thanks to George Suiter and Gary Brumfield. At the Hay cabinet shop, thanks to Marcus Hansen, Mack Headley, Dave Salisbury, and Cory Loftheim. At the cooperage, thanks to George Pettengell, Jim Pettengell, Cary Shackleford, and Lew LeCompte.

Also at Colonial Williamsburg, I am indebted to Susan Berg, Liz Ackert, Suzanne Brown, Cathy Grosfils, and Laura Arnett for their assistance at the research and audiovisual libraries. In the photographic section, thanks again to Pete Huffman, Dawn Estrin, and the director of audiovisual productions, Richard McCluney.

Among the other individuals and organizations that helped in the preparation of this book are: Frank A. Norick and the Lowie Museum of Anthropology; Rich Mally and Everett C. Wilkie, librarians at the Connecticut Historical Society; Mary Lee Allen at Gunston Hall; Charlotte Valentine at the Mariner's Museum; Bill Cuffe at the Yale University Art Gallery; Eryl Platzer at the Valentine Museum; Barbara Shattuck at the National Geographic Society; Pete Stephano at *WOOD Magazine*; and Lisa Mullins at the National Historical Society. Finally, Claire Mehalick, who has had a photo credit in each of the preceding books, appears in the photograph with the dulcimer.

"The Woodwright's Shop" began as a television series in 1979. For the great job that they have done since the beginning and at every step along the way, I want to thank Bobby Royster and the staff at the UNC Center for Public Television. If you have watched the television series, Geary Morton, director and coproducer of the series, is the man to thank for what you see.

"The Woodwright's Shop" is underwritten on PBS in large part by the State Farm Insurance Companies. All of us are grateful for their enduring support in making television safe for serious woodworking comedy.

This is also my fourth book with the University of North Carolina Press. They are quite a team and don't approve of individual thanks, for fear that someone might get left out. So, thanks to everyone. The Press building in Chapel Hill burned down while this book was underway. You all never missed a beat.

Here in the Underhill family, Jane, Rachell, and Eleanor were a tremendous help, as always, and I am very lucky to have their support and affection.

Most important, but most neglected, are all the folks who have written to me. I can't say enough how I wish that there was some way to answer all of the generous letters. I have reached the limits of my power to accomplish even half of what's on my plate. Between the work at Williamsburg, the TV series, the writing, and the family, something may eventually have to go. It's a decision I hope I never have to make. So to all of you whose letters I have not yet answered, I humbly dedicate this book.

The
Woodwright's
Eclectic
Workshop

Introduction

I had never handled a tool in my life, and yet in time, by labour, application, and contrivance, I found at last I wanted nothing but I could have made it.
– *Daniel Defoe*, Robinson Crusoe, 1719

When *Robinson Crusoe* first hit the streets in 1719, it became an instant bestseller. Since that time thousands of stories have been told and forgotten, yet this tale of a man forced to rely on simple tools and common sense has endured and is familiar to almost everyone today. What could account for its timeless appeal?

Is it just escapism? The stresses that were part of everyday life in eighteenth-century London are still with us today—with a vengeance. Could this explain the enduring popularity of the theme of "the simple life"? Is our attention to "the old ways" just more therapeutic nostalgia? No way.

The test of a classic is that it remains eternally modern. Traditional methods endure because they always have worked and they always will. Your axe will still fell a tree. Your mallet and chisel will still cut perfect dovetails. Your plane (just a block of wood with a piece of steel in it) will still give you the finest surfaces and the crispest mouldings. The old ways work; they brought us to where we are today. There *was* life before electricity.

But power tools work too, and they are readily available. Why would anyone choose to work wood with old hand tools? You might as well ask why some people prefer to travel on cross-country skis rather than snowmobiles. Both will get you there; the difference is in the character of the journey.

In this book we will learn how to make a few things in the honored tradition of the industrious amateur. We will also explore the old paths in the way that they were originally taken: not as adventuresome recreations, but as professions that put food on the table and clothes on the kids. You know their names; you may even bear one of them yourself. Who has not met a Cooper, a Charpentier, a Zimmerman, a Sawyer, a Joiner, a Zeigler, a Turner, or one of the many Wrights? But before any of these specialized trades could exist, there had to be the pioneer, the homesteader who laid the foundations of the civilization to follow. So this book begins with a little trapper's cabin.

1 Log Cabins

Most of the Houses in this Part of the Country are Log-houses, covered with Pine or Cypress Shingles, 3 feet long, and one broad. They are hung upon Laths with Peggs, and their doors too turn upon Wooden Hinges, and have wooden Locks to Secure them, so that the Building is finisht without Nails or other Iron-work.

– William Byrd, "History of the Dividing Line
   betwixt Virginia & North Carolina," 1728

Log cabins loom large in our history, both the real and the imagined. By now, most people recognize that neither the Pilgrims nor the settlers at Jamestown knew anything about log building. They knew only the building language of their native land, that of England's wattle-and-daub frame carpentry. Nor did they invent the log cabin after they had been here for a while. Many of them froze in muddy, canvas-covered holes in the ground until the Scandinavians brought their language of building with logs to the New World. Log building was a perfect fit in the new country and quickly became the dominant form on the American frontier.

As does any endeavor, log building has levels of sophistication commensurate with the time and energy that the builder can afford. Thaddeus M. Harris, in his 1805 *Journal of a Tour into the Territory Northwest of the Alleghany Mountains*, described the difference between a log cabin and a log house:

> [Cabins] are built with unhewn logs, the interstices between which are stopped with rails, calked with moss or straw, and daubed with mud. The roof is covered with a sort of thin staves split out of oak or ash, about four feet long and five inches wide, fastened on by heavy poles being laid upon them. . . . If the logs be hewed; if the interstices be stopped with stone, and neatly plastered; and the roof composed of shingle nicely laid on, it is called a log-house. A log-house has glass windows and a chimney; a cabin has commonly no window at all, and only a hole at the top for smoke to escape.

The quality of log building can mark social distinctions as well. Ernest Thompson Seton told of this in his wonderful 1903 book, *Two Little Savages*. Describing the townspeople of the fictional Canadian settlement of Sanger in the mid-nineteenth century, he wrote:

> Every man and boy in Sanger was an expert with the axe. . . . The familiar phrase, "He's a good man," . . . implied that he was unusually dexterous with the axe. A man who fell below standard was despised. Since the houses of hewn logs were made by their owners, they reflected the axeman's skill. There were two styles of log architecture; the shanty with the corners criss-cross, called hog-pen finish, and the other, the house with the corners neatly finished, called dovetail finish. In Sanger it was a social black eye to live in a house of the first kind. The residents were considered "scrubs" or "riff-raff" by those whose superior axemanship had provided the more neatly finished dwelling.

The log house that I will build with you in these pages might indeed brand you as riff-raff (but I'll still come to visit you anyway). Truly, very few of these once-common rude buildings have survived, and because of this, they are less widely understood today than the more finely finished log

houses of their time. As you build and live with such a rude cabin, you discover a sophisticated organic relationship developing between you and the materials and forces of nature. With an axe and a forest, you will see what I mean.

FELLING

To build with trees, you must first disconnect them from the ground. The axes and men that came over on the first boat were no match for the ancient giants of the American forest. But, as Benjamin Franklin noted when he watched the construction of a frontier fort in 1755, it was not long before they grew equal to the task: "Seeing the trees fall so fast, I had the curiosity to look at my watch when two men began to cut at a pine; in six minutes they had it upon the ground, and I found it of fourteen inches diameter."

By a century later in 1850, an Ohio man recalled, felling trees was considered great sport: "We experimented, as young boys will, and we felled one large hickory with the saw instead of the axe, and barely escaped with our lives when it suddenly split near the bark, and the butt shot out between us. I preferred buckeye and sycamore for my own axe; they were of no use when felled, but they chopped delightfully."

Look up, look around, and think before you begin chopping. First look for any predisposition of the tree to fall in one particular direction, caused by a lean or extended limbs. It is often better to fell the tree at right angles to the direction of the lean. You want to have cut the tree well nigh through before it goes over. You don't want to have a lot of splintering and surprises. This is dangerous business; to stay alive, you must stay in control.

The way to fell a tree with control is to hinge it down. Stand to the side of where you want the tree to fall and swing about you with the axe at full extension to be sure that there are no limbs, vines, or people to catch your axe on. Make the first cut on the side that faces the direction you want the tree to fall. You should feel as though you are whipping the axe into the tree rather than pushing it. When the first notch is more than halfway through the tree, move to the opposite side and cut the back notch a little higher up the tree than the first one. The wood that remains between these two notches is the hinge. Keep well to the side when the tree gets ready to go over. Never stand behind the falling tree; it will occasionally shoot back and can spear you like a bug.

Felling the tree is the first operation of woodworking, and the speed and ease of your axework is a prime example of one of the ☞GREAT SECRETS OF WOODWORKING☜. Examine the surface of any one of the chips that flew from the notch. When you are working at your best, the area of the chip

[opposite]
Start chopping the notch on the side where you want the tree to fall.

Make the back cut on the opposite side above the level of the first cut.

that was actually severed by the axe blade will be only about one-fifth of the total surface. The rest of the surface will plainly show that it was formed by splitting, demonstrating the extent to which you have taken advantage of the planes of weakness in the wood. This is the principle that is fundamental to the mastery of traditional woodworking:

> Exploit the weakness of the wood when you work it
> and the strength of the wood when you use it.

Good axework is the systematic process of driving in the blade to split free large chunks of wood.

Out of the Woods

If you are indeed building by yourself, without horse, helper, or handcart, you will find it unprofitable to cut a log too heavy for you to drag to the site by yourself. The tradeoff is diameter versus length. You can build a cabin wall 25 feet long if you are willing to use a lot of 4-inch-diameter logs. I figure an absolute limit is a 7-inch-diameter log that is about 14 feet long. Every tree is heavier in the butt log where it is the thickest, so that is

You may be able to carry a 14-foot log out of the woods by yourself if it is no larger than 7 inches in diameter on the small end.

the part of the tree to cut into logs for the short walls. Remember that the logs on a saddle-notched cabin must extend out beyond the corners. This requires that you cut your logs a few feet longer than the intended length of the wall.

Please don't hurt yourself doing this without adequate help. Years ago, out West, a couple had a falling-out, and the man began building a cabin on the mountaintop while the woman maintained residence in a tepee down in the aspen grove. He dragged a hundred logs up a winding path to the top of the mountain by himself, making an "I'm killing myself through log-dragging and nobody can stop me!" statement that only incidentally grew into a cabin.

Much about Bark

Bark is waterproof, which is good for the tree while it is alive and good for canoe builders, bugs, and fungi when the tree is dead. Millions of years of evolution have developed an efficient biodegradation process for recycling dead trees. If you leave the bark on a log, it will be considered part of the natural cycle by the organisms dedicated to this process. In other words, leave the bark on a log and it will rot.

The problem is not the bark itself, but the water from the living tree that the bark keeps in the log. Whether you leave the logs lying on the ground or stack them in tall, airy piles, the environment within the bark remains the same. Bugs that like to eat and nest in freshly dead trees bore through the bark and track in fungal spores that grow through the wood. This in turn attracts new bugs and more fungi that quickly destroy the log and anything you have built with it.

But what accounts for the pictures we see of houses built with logs that still have the bark on them? Surely these people knew better? Well, some did and some did not, and others didn't care. Soldiers building winter encampments cared only if their cabins would get them through the winter. They cut the logs in late fall when the insects and fungi were inactive. Come spring, if the bark was still on, the wood would still be damp inside and the bugs would come and the rot begin.

Any opening in the jacket of bark will allow the water in the log to escape as vapor. A dry log will not decay and will be much less attractive to bugs. If you remove even a strip of bark down the length of a fall-cut log, the water will escape through this opening and the log will be dry by spring. Rustic aesthetes who like the look of bark used to build dude ranches like this, hiding the bare strip under the chinking. There are also other, more expedient methods that allow you to build with bark-covered logs and still have something standing after a year.

You often see one such method in southern tobacco barns. After the logs are up, work down the length with a hatchet or axe, chopping off a 3-inch

Larger logs take more muscle and wheels to move. Garland, Dan, and Robert will place this 26-foot black locust sill on the row of decay-resistant locust-post footings. This log and its mate will be the bottommost logs in a large cabin at Carter's Grove.

wide strip on the outside and inside of each log. I once dismissed accounts of this technique, thinking that logs are only hewn before building with them. I will long remember the dismayed expression on the face of the old fellow that told me of this, when I laughed and corrected him from my extensive documentary research. Later I realized that I had photographed this technique many times without understanding the tool marks I was recording. The logs were indeed lightly hewn after the walls were up, just to help them dry out and keep them from rotting.

The funkiest technique for preserving logs is one I have also heard described, but the physical evidence for it is harder to find. This way, people interrupt the natural biological process when it reaches a point advantageous to them. There are numerous other such examples in human endeavors. Flax is rotted until it is soft enough work into linen. Sweet potatoes are allowed to cure (dry) until it's safe to store them in the root cellar. Wild game is hung for a time before being cut up. All of these practices involve interrupting a natural process at just the right time. Too soon, and it won't have any helpful effect. Too late, and the stuff will spoil. So, too, the log builder can wait until the inevitable bugs loosen the bark so that it can be pulled off by hand. With the bark off, the bugs leave and the logs dry before the fungi can do serious damage. The logs don't look pretty, but once dry, they will last.

The most fastidious means of getting the bark off is to peel the entire log. Peeling the bark off logs will give you plenty of opportunity to con-

The tobacco barn behind this North Carolina farm family was laid up from small, bark-covered pine logs. After the walls were up, each log was lightly hewn down its length to remove a 3-inch-wide strip of bark and wood. This hewing allowed the logs to dry in place before the insects and decay could attack them. (It was not the custom to smile for the camera in 1903.)

[left]
In the spring and early summer you can peel the bark from a log with an iron barking spud.

[right]
In the fall and winter, or on a log that is too dry, a drawknife is the best tool for removing bark.

template your misdeeds. Skinning a tree, like skinning a deer, gets you covered with blood. The sap sprays onto your skin and hair, then grabs all the dust in the air and sticks it all to you. Although the long-handled barking spud is best for peeling larger logs, smaller logs are easier to peel with a drawknife. A tree with a crook, crotch, or branch at about shoulder height makes a convenient lodgement for the pole being peeled. You will last even longer if you can perch the log horizontally about waist high. At least one of the supports should be V-shaped to keep curved logs from rolling back to their favored hanging position.

If you don't mind the solitude, you may find it wiser to peel your logs in the woods so you won't have to clean up bark. Be warned that a fresh-peeled log is slipperier than owl spit and is better left to dry a few days before you haul it out. The drier it gets the lighter it gets.

SQUARING

Often you will feel the need to flatten your log on at least two sides before you use it. This need for squaring is only partially based on the neurotic western-European compulsion to impose strict geometric order on natural forms. Shaping the log into a standard rectangular section is genuinely helpful in the systematic construction of a frame building. It also gives you the flat walls for the more polite forms of log building. It gives you a lighter, stiffer timber and most certainly allows the log to dry. Squaring a log is generally useful and you need to know how to do it.

Layout

Although you can do the squaring entirely by eye, even the most experienced workers usually place guidelines on the log before going at it with an axe. First, roll the log up off the ground onto two short cross-logs with notches cut in their tops so that the log will not rock about. If the log curves, orient it so that the curve hangs in the vertical plane rather than to one side. Sit down at the small end of the log with a plumb bob, a scratch awl, and a square and begin the layout. At the top of your end of the log, spear the end grain twice with the scratch awl to mark out the thickness that you want to hew the timber to. From each of these two points, drop the plumb line and mark the lower end. With the square and awl, scribe vertical lines that connect the top and bottom points. Get up, go to the other end, and do the same thing.

Once you have the two ends marked out, connect them down the length of the log with a snapline. You can use the charcoal of willow wood rubbed on the string, or pokeberry juice, but chalk is as old as the White Cliffs of Dover. When you snap the line, be sure to strain it in the same plane as the surface that you want to create. If you mistakenly pull out radially from the heart of the log, the odd contours of the natural surface will throw your line way off.

Hewing

Hewing is a means of getting what you want by chopping off what you don't need. Almost all of the wood is removed by splitting. Ideally, you could drive in a wedge at one end of the log and split off the whole side at once. Realistically though, you will have to shorten the length of the piece to be split off. The way to do this is to stand on top of the log and chop a series of notches into the side down to the line. Space these notches about a foot apart unless you come to a knot, in which case you must chop in right atop it. You then swing down with the grain and split off the chunks

To mark guidelines on the log for more precise hewing, stretch out a string, rub it with charcoal, hold it tight at each end and snap it in the middle.

To hew off lots of wood, Garland chops in notches across the grain to the line as Bill swings in along the grain to split off the chunks between the notches.

The broad axe shaves down across the grain to leave a smooth, accurate finish. The bent handle keeps your fingers attached to your hands as you work.

between the notches. (This is why you must get rid of the knots; otherwise they would peg the chunk firmly to the log.) Continue on down the log until all of the chunks are split off.

At this point, the hewn surface is quite rough. You can further level it by chopping a more closely spaced array of scorings and then again splitting along the grain. The finishing touch is to slice down across the grain of the timber. This can be done with the felling axe, but the specialized broad axe makes the job much easier. The broad axe has a face that is virtually flat on the side toward the log. The handle is generally offset to the opposite side so that your fingers will remain attached to your hands as you work. When one side is done you do the opposite side and continue to make the log foursquare.

BUILDING THE WALLS

Getting the materials ready to build implies that you have a location picked out. Locate in haste, repent at leisure. So many factors go into this important decision that only time spent at the site can bring them all into focus. Camp out as long as possible at the site to see how it meshes with the wind, the sun, the view, the drainage, the neighbors, and the distance to water.

A cabin with a dirt floor may or may not have a foundation. A low skirt of brick or stone can support the outer walls above the damp and decay of the ground. The inside can be filled with packed earth to make a good floor. Often, though, a cabin is built with groundsills or "mudsills" that lie directly on the ground. As long as these bottommost logs are of extremely decay-resistant wood such as locust, heart pine, or cypress, they will last long enough to give you the option of installing more permanent foundations. Old country builders' records are filled with mentions of "underpinning" buildings—lifting them up and putting new brick beneath.

Set the sill logs parallel to and level with one another. (For a cabin, they're right when they look right.) For a log house with a wooden floor, these timbers need to be squared and leveled carefully to hold the floor joists. Sill logs usually go on the long walls of the cabin, but if you are going to make the door opening on the shorter, gable end, you may wish to place the sills on the short ends also to keep the threshold from being too high.

Saddle Notching

Saddle notches are generally deemed the least sophisticated of the many forms of corner joints for log buildings. You simply chop a hollow near the end of a log to match the contour of the one it crosses. Just because saddle notches are simple does not mean they have to be roughly done. But because they are simple, they are most often chosen for buildings of expediency.

You can quickly learn to cut a saddle notch by setting the log in place and chopping, by eye, the mirror image of the log beneath it into its top side. Do the same at the far end and roll the log over into place. The deeper you chop the notch, the closer the top log will drop toward the one beneath it. Depending on how deep you cut the notch, you can build a cabin with no gaps at all, or one that needs lots of chinking and daubing to close the spaces between the logs.

You may well find it neater and easier in the long run to use a pair of dividers to scribe the notches. All you need to do is open the dividers to the desired depth of the notch and, keeping them vertical, pull them

around the proposed joint. The bottom leg of the dividers rides over the bottom log as the top leg scratches this contour into the side of the top log. You may reset the dividers a little wider to make a log drop a little more on one end, but do not let the log get jostled before both ends have been marked.

As the first course of logs goes into place, you can start exercising the judgment that will keep the walls rising evenly. Most logs are going to be thicker on one end than on the other. If you put all the thick ends at one corner, that corner will tend to rise faster than the others. The obvious solution is to alternate fat and skinny ends to keep the rise even. You will also find it wise to use your heavier logs first. Now too is the time to square the building by measuring for equal diagonals between the corners if you feel so compelled.

As the walls rise, you may need to place long skid poles against the walls to help you raise the logs. A block and tackle anchored to the far wall or the common parbuckle arrangement will enable you to move the heaviest logs. Working solo, I have had the best luck simply using the skids to allow me to slide up one end at time. When one end of the log is as high

[left]

You can chop a saddle notch entirely by eye, or you can precisely scribe the joint by drawing a pair of dividers so that the bottom point rides on the lower log as the upper point marks the upper log. Do the same on the back side of the log and then carefully do the other end of the log. Be careful to keep the points of the dividers in plumb vertical alignment as you scribe, and don't bump the logs before you're done.

[right]

When the scribing is complete, roll the log back over and chop to the line with a light axe.

Roll the log back into place and it should fit perfectly. Set the dividers wider to make a deeper notch that will close up the gap between the logs.

as I can push it, I anchor it with a rope and move the other end into place. You can keep your skids on one side of the building if you always roll up the log intended for the opposite wall first and roll it across the top of the pen into place.

The walls can rise pretty fast when everything is going your way, but this can be mighty hard work on a hot day. Once, working on a large cabin, we managed to get only two courses of logs into place on a day that reached 105° in the shade. We were not in the shade. On a normal day we could get up eight to twelve courses in a day.

When the walls reach the height of the ceiling space that you need for the ground level, it's time to set on the joists. These joists span the narrow width at regular intervals and will both support the loft space and create whatever eaves overhang you might require. If you are making a rafter roof, these extended joists will support the plate that in turn supports the rafter feet.

Openings

Anyone wandering by at this time might feel compelled to point out that you have forgotten to make a door into your cabin. You might also feel compelled to bounce the palm of your hand off your forehead and say "Darn! I knew there was something wrong." Now that the walls are up, before the roof goes on, it is time to cut the door and window openings. Mark the openings and nail split saplings around them to keep the logs in place until the door is cut and framed.

You can start the crosscut saw at the top of the proposed opening by several methods. You can saw partway through the log at the top corner of the opening as you are laying up the wall. If you wait until the walls are

up to decide where the doors and windows will go, you can chop through the top log of the opening with an axe. With big, thick, hard logs, you can make the chopping easier by boring a vertical row of auger holes along the line of the opening. Chopping into this row from the waste side will quickly give you an opening for the crosscut saw. I have found this method used to cut new doors through a walnut and oak cabin in Illinois dating from 1850.

Continue laying up the logs until you are obliged to saw a door opening to get inside. The saplings nailed to either side of the door opening keep the logs from falling and pinching the saw blade. The roof of this little cabin is well underway. The joists extend outward on the front and back walls to keep the rain clear of the clay daubing that will help fill the gaps between the logs.

Pegging in the Jambs

Split or hew the inch-and-a-half-thick doorjambs to frame the interior of the door openings. Nails or common pegs won't hold well in the end grain of logs, so here is where you commonly find "fox" or blind wedging handy to make the pegs hold. After boring a hole through the jamb and into the end grain of the log, all you need do is split the end of the peg and insert a wedge into the split before you drive in the peg. When the wedge hits the bottom of the auger hole in the log, it will expand the peg like a dumdum bullet. Cut off the protruding end of the peg, split it with a chisel across the grain of the jamb, and drive in another wedge.

If your logs are still fresh and green, remember that they are going to shrink as they dry. In a log house, where the height is determined entirely

Frame the door opening with heavy planks pegged into the end grain of the logs. Orient the wedges in the ends of the pegs as they are here to exert pressure along the grain of the plank, not across it. Wedging the other way would split the plank.

Before I went to build the cabin by the lake, I made a list of tools that I would need. They proved to be more than enough:

felling axe	*froe club*
hatchets	*dividers*
adz	*gimlets*
brace and bits	*knife*
crosscut saw	*shovel*
1-man crosscut	*hoe*
bucksaw	*bucket*
wedges	*drawknives*
maul	*broad axe*
froe	

by the cross grain of the wood, this can add up to a lot of movement. People usually advise you to let the cabin "settle" before you install any vertical elements such as door and window jambs. If you install jambs in a green log wall, you can make room for the settling by cutting the notches in the head log (the one you hit your head on when you go in the door) about 2 inches deeper than they need to be. The jambs need to be stoutly affixed because they will take the weight of the door, but for now, just nail up a blanket and get a roof on the place before you bother with the door.

THE ROOF

There are two basic ways to put a gable roof on the cabin. The first is to use conventional carpentered rafters built in the form of giant capital A's. These rafters sit on or notch over the plate held by the ends of the joists. First covered with thin shingle laths or "nailers," the rafters are finally covered over with nailed-on shingles. The second, apparently older method completes the entire structure using the language of log building from bottom to top. With this method, you build up log gables with lengthwise purlins that gradually converge at the peak. This roof is typically much lower in pitch and is covered with long boards held down by weight poles lying on top of them.

Once you start making this latter form of roof from increasingly shorter gable-end logs and the long purlin logs, you will need to change the way

Trim down the ends of the gable-end logs with an axe or adz. Note that the purlins (the long logs), are notched top and bottom in the roof framing. The flush-trimmed gable-end logs would not have enough meat left on them to hold if they were notched.

Garland splits a prime red oak log into billets that are light enough to carry out of the woods. These will be split further to make the boards for the roof.

you notch. Instead of notching the underside of the gable-end logs to cup down over the purlins, you must notch the purlins both top and bottom. This has two advantages. First, it allows you to move the purlins in and out to bring them into the same plane before you lay the roof. Second, it maintains the notching that would otherwise be chopped away when you trim the gable-end logs to the line of the roof. Saddle-notched logs need a good length beyond the corner to maintain their grip. Since only the purlin logs can extend beyond this corner, only they can be notched.

Leave the gable-end logs long until you have reached the peak and have knocked the purlins back and forth into a single plane. The roof boards that lie on this plane will foot against a butting pole pegged to the ends of the joists. Lay a board on the purlins and see that they are indeed aligned as you hope. When you are sure you have the alignment as you need it, chop the ends of the gable-end logs off flush with the rest of the roof. A sharp adz makes this job considerably easier.

Riving

Although your roof could be covered with hewn planks or even sawn boards, the most durable roof is made from riven clapboards. Choose your riving trees with care. Some, like elm or gum, can barely be split with gunpowder. Others that ordinarily do well, like oak, cypress, or pine, may be so knotty or twisted as to be useless for better work. You can split fence rails or building studs from such stuff, but clapboards and shingles that need to be flat and smooth can only be made from very big, very old trees.

Knots, the buried stubs of low branches overgrown by new wood, await you in the core of almost every tree. The grain of the wood flows around these obstructions like water around rocks in a rushing stream. But the longer and larger the tree grows, the more the wood becomes like a deep, flowing river—straighter, clearer, and more workable. You must learn to "read" the tree for the signs of these flaws, which show up as irregularities or spiraling in the bark.

Work the timber while it is still fresh. Wood works much more easily when it is green, requiring only about two-thirds as much effort to split it as when it is dry. In addition, a log left lying around for very long is considered fair game by the bugs. Even the nicest-looking shingles won't last very long if they are full of woodworm holes.

Once the tree is on the ground and has been crosscut to the appropriate lengths, split the cylinder down the middle by driving in an iron wedge near the edge of one end until the crack begins. Once started, the split may be continued by using "gluts"—wedges made from dogwood or other tough stuff. Once the log is in half, continue to halve each of the pieces until they all match the thickness of your upper arm. This is the size best worked by the long-handled wedge most commonly known as the froe.

The Froe

The froe leads two lives. When you drive the dull blade into the end grain of the wood, it works like a wedge. Once driven in to the point where you can't strike it with the club any more, the froe becomes a lever, enabling you to continue the split down the length of the wood by pushing or pulling the long handle to one side or the other. This simple leverage gives you the strength of ten.

Splitting wood may seem to be a "wild" process that, once begun, is uncontrollable. Splitting does tend to follow the natural grain of the wood, and this is one of the great advantages of the process. The strength of the grain is kept intact, and the surfaces created are less permeable to water. To some extent, however, you can control the direction of the split as it progresses. By bending one side of the wood more than the other, you may redirect the split to that side. For shingles, oak is best split radially, across the growth rings. Cypress is just the opposite and should be riven out "flat," or tangential to the rings.

A big forked limb, sometimes called a riving break, will help you bend the wood to direct the split. As you work the froe down the length of the wood, place the thicker side down and push on it to give it an extra bend. You need this control to avoid ruining a piece by having the split prematurely "run out" to one side. This is good work. Even Albert Einstein once commented, "Everyone likes to split wood—one sees the results immediately."

When the pieces are as thin as you want them to be, they will often need additional trimming with a hatchet to remove the decay-prone white sapwood under the bark. They may also need some shaving with a draw-knife to ensure that they will lie flat and tight on the roof or walls. The finished boards then go into great tall stacks to dry and flatten a bit before they go on the house. The rejects go into the fire, inspiring the expression, "The good ones keep you dry, and the bad ones keep you warm."

Lay these boards in a single flat course on the roof purlins so that they rest against the butting pole. Now go down the length of the roof laying on another course that covers the gaps in the first one. Saw some poles into short lengths or "knees" to support the next weight pole about halfway up the length of the first layer of boards. Lay on this weight pole and use it as the butting pole for the next course of boards. The length of the knees and the number of weight poles that you use depends on the size of your roof, the length of your boards, and the degree of overlap that you want. These weight poles are directly exposed to the weather and will need to be checked for rot every few years. I assure you that this cabin is intended to pass the Code of the Wilderness and no other.

The froe leads two lives. Here I drive the froe in like a wedge to start the split. Notice that I have released the handle of the froe with my left hand to protect it from the transmitted shock of the blow from the hickory club. I was not aware of this habit until I saw this photograph.

Once driven in, the froe works as a lever to move the split down the wood. The big forked limb here is called a riving break. It allows you to control the direction of the split by pushing down and putting an extra bend on the thicker piece. This causes the split to run back to the middle.

[above]

The roof boards in this type of roof butt against a pole pegged to the top ends of the joists. Each course consists of two layers of boards, the top layer covering the gaps between the boards beneath.

[left]

The low pitch of the roof allows the boards to be held in place by the weight of the poles and rocks rather than by expensive nails.

The strap of this wooden hinge extends across the door boards to help act as a batten. Boring the eye for the pintle through a knot in the wood makes the strongest hinge.

[opposite]
Split the pintle from dogwood and shave it down with a knife.

HINGES AND LATCHES

Wooden hinges are fun to make; they're Frank's favorites due to his strongly developed drive for gathering gnarly wood. When splitting oak shingles or whatever, Frank always sets aside pieces in which knots have pulled out of the wood at one end. This leaves a piece where the grain flows around a hole that he did not have to bore. Flattened on one face, these pieces with the holes become the strap hinges for doors and shutters.

Because these wooden strap hinges can be as long as the door is wide, they may also serve as battens to join the split or sawn planks that make up the doors. The door boards can be butted together and the gaps covered with another layer of boards, as on the roof, or with narrower vertical battens. To add strength, the nails that hold the door together can extend through and be clinched back "dead as a doornail."

You can very quickly chop the pintles for these hinges from an ox-bone-sized piece of fresh dogwood. Saw out a section about a handspan long. Split it lengthwise to make a flat surface to spike against the walls of the cabin. Now chop across this face at the point where you want the shoulder of the pintle, chop in on the sides, split down from the ends, whittle it round, and trim the bottom to a nice diminuendo. Sometimes you see these pintles left long so that they can be nailed back to the jamb. Wooden hinges like these are common in smokehouses, where the salt used for curing hams would quickly eat away iron hinges.

"Latchstring?"

"Yes, latchstring. I had to go out myself to find out what the darn thing is. There's a latch on the inside of the door, with a string tied to it. When you want to let somebody just walk in, you stick the little string through a hole in the door, so the string dangles outside. If you don't want people walking in, you pull the string in through the hole. Ghastly?"

"I'll survive somehow. Is the latchstring out?" (Kurt Vonnegut, Player Piano, 1952)

CHINKING AND DAUBING

Chinking and daubing are two different things. Chinking consists of solid blocks of wood or stone that you drive into the spaces between the logs. Most convenient are the triangular sectioned pieces left from splitting clapboards. The random gaps need a good selection of random chinking material. Drive the pieces in with the butt of your axe until they sound solid. Daubing is the mud or clay plaster that makes the final seal. Straw mixed in with the plaster will act as a binder to keep the clay together as it dries. Adding lime and manure to the mix will make the daubing more durable in all weather. There is no way to get the daubing in except by applying it directly with your hands, so watch for splinters. Try to undercut the daubing so that rainwater will run over the outside rather than down under it.

This little cabin is roofed with sawn boards and capped at the ridge. The wide gaps between the logs are chinked with wood and daubed with clay.

This 1791 sketch of a Creek Indian cabin in northern Georgia or Alabama shows a stick-and-clay chimney that holds close to the gable-end wall for its whole length.

Stick-and-clay chimneys often lean out from the building and sometimes even have to be supported by long poles.

FIREPLACE AND CHIMNEY

You might think that a fireplace and chimney must be made from brick or stone, but this assumes that you have brick or stone available and know how to work with them. There is a marvelous type of chimney that uses the same language and materials as the rest of the building. The earliest illustration I know of this type of stick-and-mud or "cat-and-clay" chimney dates from 1791 and shows Creek Indians at home (in a house that originated in Finland).

The firebox will someday catch fire or rot and will need to be rebuilt, so don't try to lay up a log firebox as you build the rest of the cabin. Notch only the outer corners of the firebox logs and join the free ends to the wall of the cabin by chopping them down to a taper that will fit into the gaps between the wall logs. When the firebox reaches sufficient height, you can cut an opening through the wall as you did for the door.

Above the firebox, the chimney begins as a narrowing pen of smaller logs and then continues upward as a regular column of heavy sticks. Clay is a key ingredient of this structure, because any exposed wood will eventually catch fire. The firebox needs at least a 6-inch-thick lining of clay. The chimney can do with a thinner coating, but it has a harder job staying in place. The best way to get a solid and firm coating of clay is to see that it has sufficient binder and that it is keyed to both the outside and inside surfaces as you build up the sticks. From your supply of foot-mixed muck, roll four long sausages and lay them on top of the row of sticks. Lay on another course of sticks and another course of sausages in alternation until you have gone up about a foot. Now take extra clay as needed and smooth

and blend the clay that has extruded from the sides. Your chimney will soon be the envy of the neighborhood.

The curious thing about the stick chimney is its reaction to humidity. Remember that wood expands and contracts a great deal *across* the grain but hardly any *along* the grain. Think about the way an 18-foot-tall crib of oak sticks is going to behave. It will grow or shrink by about 4 percent with changes in the weather. This means the chimney has the potential of growing 9 inches higher after a rainstorm. As long as the chimney is free to move, no harm is done. But the slower-responding, drier cabin stays relatively still. If the chimney contacts the edge of the roof, the two will grind against each other until the chimney is torn apart. The best course is to have the chimney stand free of the walls—both for safety in case of fire and to keep the chimney intact.

Often in pictures we see a pole propping up stick-and-clay chimneys. This pole could keep a leaning chimney from falling over or could be used to push a burning one away from the house. Another common practice is to extend the gable of the roof over the chimney to protect it from the rain. In any case, constant maintenance is part of the deal. This is a very different, organic relationship with your house. For now, though, your work is done. Now it's time to go inside, sit down, and I will tell you one of my stories.

No matter how well stick-and-clay chimneys are made, the clay coating must be constantly maintained, or the bare wood will catch fire and perhaps take the rest of the house with it.

BUILT TO LAST

Dan Cory was mighty proud of the old log walls of his new den. He discovered them beneath the plaster in the kitchen of the old family home. He loved to stand by the fire, scotch in hand, and hold forth to family and friends about the virtues of simpler times. "Look at these logs, over a hundred years old! People built things to last back then! Shows what you can do when you take your time to do things right!"

Anna Cory, Dan's great-grandmother, was not thinking about taking her time back in April 1884 when she stood in that very spot. Around her there were only eighty acres of pine woods and a mule hitched to a wagon that stood where Anna's daughter Nan sat looking over her father's grave. They had no house, no barns, no cleared fields, nor anyone around to help them; but they had axes, a saw, and trees.

It took Anna and Nan all of that first day to fell just ten small pines and cut them to length. By pivoting the logs about their midpoint and lifting one end at a time, they wrestled the bottom pair of logs into place on the ground. Anna knew that the groundsills of a log house ought to be of locust or chestnut—pine would not last two years on the ground—but she had no time for niceties. She just wanted the two of them to make it through the oncoming winter.

The women moved the next pair of logs so that they spanned the ends of the first pair—and stopped. They knew that they had to notch the ends of the logs to hold them in place, but they didn't know how. They tried to picture the dovetail notches that they had seen the men make. They tried to trace them out in the dirt, but they never came out right. Finally Anna said, "I don't have time to figure out these dovetails. I'm just going to chop some hollows for that end log to lie in."

Anna eyed the contour of the end log and pictured how it should set down into the log below it. She rolled the log out of the way and chopped its contour into the end of the bottom log. Without stopping to rest, she rolled the log back into place. Nan watched with a worried eye. "Daddy told me that you always fit wood together so that it sheds the rain. Those cradle-cuts are gonna catch the rain and rot." "Baby," her mother puffed, "we're gonna be the ones that rot if we don't get a roof over our heads. You get back to cutting trees. We've got to plant tomorrow."

Each night they climbed over the growing walls to sleep on the ground within the doorless box of brown-barked pine logs. Later Anna spiked split poplar saplings to the walls on either side of where she wanted the door. With the logs held in place, she chopped an opening to make room to start the crosscut saw. The two women worked the saw downward, jumping back when the short sections of log fell free. The door opening, covered with a red blanket, lifted their tired spirits; their pen of logs was beginning to seem like a real house, awaiting only a roof to make it complete.

[opposite]
A cabin near Richmond, Virginia, built by a mother and daughter.

The corn was two feet high when the noise began. At first there was just a faint clicking in one log, but every night the nibbling host multiplied. A growing din of "click, crunch, crunch, click" surrounded the exhausted women. Holes appeared in the bark and emitted showers of sawdust that fell directly onto their faces no matter where they moved to sleep. Tired as they were, the gnawing bugs were about to drive them insane. In desperation, Anna grabbed a worn-out mule shoe by one end. She struck at the source of the nearest noise and knocked free a sheet of warm, damp, worm-riddled bark. In a fury known only to tired people denied their rest, they tore the worm-loosened bark from the walls. The musty smell that had filled the cabin soon went away, and the bare log surfaces cracked as they dried, leaving them scarred, stained, and dusty but protected from further attack.

Gradual prosperity brought changes to the hovel in the pines. That winter Anna and Nan added a fireplace and chimney of mud-covered sticks. By the following winter, the sill logs were rotten, but they enlisted help from their neighbors to lever the whole cabin up and underpin it with fieldstone. After another few years they covered the outside of the logs with sawn boards. Eventually the inside walls were plastered over, and the original log cabin became the kitchen for a new frame house. No one knew about the logs hidden in the walls until Dan discovered them during an infuriating attempt at rewiring.

"Look at those logs!" he would say. "Been there a hundred years! They built things to last back then. Shows you what you can do when you're not in a hurry."

AXEMAKER

Weapon shapely, naked, wan,
Head from the mother's bowels drawn,
Wooded flesh and metal bone,
Limb only one and lip only one,
Gray-blue leaf by red-heat grown,
Helve produced from a little seed sown,
Resting the grass amid and upon,
To be lean'd and to lean on.
– Walt Whitman, "Song of the Broad-Axe," 1892

Like most woodworkers, I know the toolsmith through his work: the axe with "perfect balance," the chisel that "really holds an edge." Rick Guthrie made an axe for me, folding an iron bar to form the body and welding in tool steel to form the bit. Once you have been present at the birth of an axe, you will never take one for granted again.

Rick folds the butterfly of iron to form the eye and blade of the hand axe.

Design

First, with marks of fireproof soapstone, Rick outlines on the cold iron bar the area that he will spread and thin to form the eye of the axe. This axe will not be the result of casual estimation; it will follow a specific transitional form of the eighteenth century, halfway between the old English axe and the new American felling axe with its heavy "poll" on the side opposite the bit. This axe will have only a slight poll but full "lugs" or "ears" descending on either side of the eye. These triangular reinforcements (if that is what they are) will strengthen the handle from side to side yet maintain flex in the line of the swing.

Forging

Into the fire it goes, centered in the jet blast of the bellows-blown coal fire. Rick probes, watching for the bright yellow heat. From the rack on the front of the brick forge he chooses his tongs from among more than a dozen. The leverage afforded by these tongs will enable him to hold and control the glowing iron with one hand as he strikes with his hammer in the other.

Fast from the fire it comes to the center of the anvil. The fading heat leaves Rick no time for hesitation. With his cross-peen hammer, he strikes the middle of the iron bar to thin and spread it, forming what will become the wraparound hole for the handle or eye of the axe. Rick does not work alone. To speed the work, a "striker" stands by to follow the blows of the hand hammer with strikes from a heavy sledge. The striker follows Rick's lead, blow for blow—"bink-BANK! bink-BANK!"—until a stop is signaled with a tap to the face or side of the anvil. After a quick survey of the work and a few refining strikes, Rick swings the iron back to the fire for the second heating.

Out of the fire it comes again. This time, for more precision than can be mustered with a free-swung blow, Rick chooses a "set hammer," a stamp on a slender handle. The striker now swings his sledge to hit the set hammer at each point that Rick determines. Set and strike, set and strike, they work until the eye takes the form and symmetry of a butterfly with wings unfolded. Before the redness fades, they bend the iron around to close the eye, folding the wings together in preparation for welding. Back into the fire it goes.

Welding

Whereas, before, the iron was molded at yellow heat, now Rick prepares the fire, making it cleaner and deeper for the white heat of welding. If luck occurs when opportunity and preparation meet, then all successful

[opposite]
Sparks fly from the joint as Rick hammer-welds the white-hot iron together around the inserted steel cutting bit.

welds are "lucky." The metal will fuse only when the surfaces are carefully prepared and then brought together at precisely the right instant. To form the molecular bond, the iron must be almost white-hot. But such heat also promotes the formation of surface oxides, gray flaky scales that get sandwiched in the joint and prevent the molecules from bonding. To stop these oxides from forming, Rick protects the iron from the atmosphere of the fire with a glassy coating of molten flux—sand or borax that melts when it comes in contact with the hot iron. When he drives the surfaces together with the sledge, the molten flux will be forced to the outside of the joint, allowing the bare iron surfaces to meet and join as one.

Once again, hot from the fire it comes, its liquid surface heated almost to the point of burning up like a July Fourth sparkler. Without wasting an instant, Rick centers it on the anvil, and smith and striker shut the joint with alternating blows. The incandescent flux sprays out the sides in electric yellow showers. The force of the blows not only welds the iron together but begins the spreading and shaping of the bit end of the axe head.

Steel

The iron from which Rick has forged the body of the axe is tough and strong but too soft to hold a cutting edge for very long. The axe must now have its tool steel bit inserted and welded into place. Rick and his striker split open the business end of the axe head, spread it apart, and "tooth" it to give it a better bite into the steel. With the steel bit positioned in the iron, Rick slowly brings the head to welding heat, carefully watching for the overheating that would burn and ruin the steel. At white heat he brings it out to the anvil and drives the joint shut, welding and shaping it under the blows of the two hammers.

Tempering

Tool steel is an especially useful mixture of iron and carbon, not only because it can be hardened but because its degree of hardness can be controlled. After bringing the cutting end of the axe head to a cherry red heat, Rick takes it from the fire and plunges it into the brine of the quench tub. The sudden cooling causes the steel to form a crystalline structure so hard that a file would skate off it as if it were glass.

Too hard and too brittle to use, the steel must now be tempered by careful reheating to modify its molecular arrangement. Rick uses the residual heat in the unquenched body of the axe to accomplish this reheating. As soon as the heat glow disappears from the cutting edge, he pulls the steaming metal from the water. Quickly polishing a portion of the cutting edge with a rub of sandstone, he watches the bright surface for the changing oxidation colors that indicate the increase in temperature as the heat

returns. First a yellow hue appears and then gradually turns to brown. When this brown becomes tinged with shades of purple, Rick plunges the axe back into the brine, fixing the temper. The axe is now hard enough to hold a razor edge, yet tough enough to chop oak knots.

With file and grindstone, Rick now adds refinements and a bright finish to the dull gray of the forged iron. He examines it closely for flaws before handing it to me. "Let me know if you have any problems with it," he says. The axe is beautiful.

The finished hand axe, ground and polished, with a hickory helve.

HENRY, GO SOAK YOUR HEAD!

Near the end of March, 1845, I borrowed an axe and went down to the woods by Walden Pond.
– Henry David Thoreau, Walden, *1854*

Even if you know nothing else about Henry David Thoreau, you probably recall that he took to the woods, built a one-room cabin, and advised us to "simplify, simplify." The story of his two years and two months in his cabin by the pond became his great work, *Walden*. But in spite of his philosophical gifts, Thoreau was also a terror. Thoreau was the bane of all working men. Thoreau was a tool borrower!

He started by borrowing the most personal and elemental of tools—another man's axe: "The owner of the axe, as he released his hold on it, said that it was the apple of his eye; but I returned it sharper than I received it."

Well, thanks for sharpening it, Henry, but did you have to ruin the handle? Henry had just begun felling pines when the axe head worked loose. He cut a new hickory wedge, drove it in with a stone, and then he made the fatal move. He "placed the whole to soak in a pond-hole in order to swell the wood."

No, Henry! Soaking the handle to swell the wood in the eye of the axe to keep it tight may seem like a good idea, but it quickly backfires. The water swells the hickory handle and locks it tight in the iron head, but the swelling is so powerful that the wood cells are crushed. When the wood dries, the crushed cells shrink to a size considerably smaller than before the soaking, and the handle is looser than ever. Leave your axe out in the rain a few times and you will discover the same thing.

But, loose axe head or not, Henry kept working, preparing the timbers for his cabin. "I hewed the main timbers six inches square, most of the studs on two sides only, and the rafters and floor timbers on one side, leaving the rest of the bark on, so that they were just as straight and much stronger than sawed ones."

Thoreau knew the value and strength of simplicity. The round timbers were stronger, if heavier, than rectangular pieces. And, by hewing one side, he not only created a flat surface to nail to, but he also ensured that his work would last more than just a few years. Flattening one side of the poles allowed the wood to dry and season so that it would not rot or be eaten by bugs. Although we think of a cabin in the woods as being a log cabin, Thoreau actually built a tiny, 10-by-15-foot frame house with lath-and-plaster walls. He had developed his skills as a carpenter the year before when he helped his father build the family house. He also learned from whom to borrow more tools: "Each stick was carefully mortised or tenoned by its stump, for I had borrowed other tools by this time."

So somebody's auger, mallet, square, chisel, and rule weren't there when they were needed. Imagine going out to fix the cowshed and reaching into your tool box only to discover that the loony by the lake had been there before you. No wonder Thoreau's cabin cost him only 28 dollars, 12½ cents. No wonder "the mass of men lead lives of quiet desperation"—the poets have borrowed all their tools.

But Henry reveled in the work. "Shall we forever resign the pleasure of construction to the carpenter?" His philosophical writing became peppered with woodworking imagery: "Drive a nail home and clinch it so faithfully that you can wake up in the night and think of your work with satisfaction."

By that August, Henry had returned the borrowed axe. To replace it, he found "an old axe which nobody claimed." With this orphan blade, he chopped the stumps out of his bean field for firewood. Striking through dirt and rock quickly ruined the tool. Small wonder that this work inspired his best-known maxim. Splitting the stumps, Henry tells us, "warmed me twice,—once while I was splitting them, and again when they were on the fire."

If no one claimed the axe before, those few weeks of stump grubbing sealed its fate. The grit wore out the bit and the impact spread the eye of the axe. A friend advised Henry to have the village blacksmith repair it, but Henry skipped the smith and, "putting in a hickory helve from the woods into it, made it do. If it was dull, it was at least hung true."

Perhaps Henry did return his borrowed axe sharper than when he received it. And perhaps he did learn to make a good handle for the one he found. Henry learned as he worked, and he had a few things to teach us as well. He became the greatest of all American philosophers, whose works have inspired millions. But never let us forget it was that borrowed axe, the generosity of some trusting woodworker, that made it all possible.

So let that be a lesson to you.

THE WOODLOT

It is remarkable what a value is still put upon wood, a value more permanent and universal than that of gold.
– Henry David Thoreau, Walden, 1854

Not many North Americans drive oxen these days, but Martha-Mac hardly gave it a thought. I could barely keep up with her as she guided the beasts and their sledge up the hill between the trees. We were cutting wood on land that had been tended by her family for five generations. She had moved back to the farm after the death of her father. "Better drop that

maple." She pointed to a 10-inch-thick tree with a weeping brown scar where its bark joined the Pennsylvania hillside.

The chips that fell from my axe showed dark stains where the wood had decayed. She picked up one of the larger chips, peeled it apart, and studied its grain. "Straight stuff—too bad," she said, tossing the chip back to the ground. "I'm getting good money for curly maple gunstocks. Straight-grained stuff this size is only good for firewood." "Why not just leave it?" I asked, giving the axe a well-deserved rest. "Bad investment. It's taking space from the younger trees around it."

We loaded the maple on the sledge, leaving only the uppermost branches. I pointed to the remaining brush. "At least we brought all of those buds and twigs down to where the deer can reach them."

Martha-Mac was not so sentimental. "Those deer tear this place up when they're hungry." She walked on up the hill, stopping now and then to feel the bark of an oak, to study the lean of a black cherry, or to knock the dead branches from a red cedar. By the time I joined her, she had picked out another five deformed, damaged, or decrepit trees for the firewood pile.

Deer were not the only unwelcome visitors to her forest. Every few years a timber buyer would make his way up the valley. He would pop his gum and offer Martha-Mac a few hundred dollars for "that patch of timber on the hill"—provided, of course, that he could come in and cut everything. She was always as polite as a lady with a Winchester could be.

Martha-Mac intended to keep her forest. Her family had cut and sold prime furniture-grade cherry, walnut, oak, tulip poplar, and hard maple from this land for two centuries. Her people could find a market for anything. Before World War I, they had sold winter-cut hickory saplings to rustic furniture makers. In the spring they peeled hickory bark to sell for chair bottoms. They sold second-growth ash and hickory for handle stock. Her father claimed that he won the World Series every year with the 40-inch-long bolts of ash that he sold to the baseball bat factory.

Even obscure species could turn a profit for her family. They sold soft, decay-resistant sassafras for ox yokes, dense persimmon for golf club heads, smooth-wearing dogwood for industrial weaving shuttles, and even some of the light but tough willow down by the pond to make artificial arms and legs. In recent years, Martha-Mac had put aside burls and other curious wood for bowl turners, and every December she cut and sold mistletoe and holly.

Much of the odd timber from the woodlot had been used for fencing. There was always a need for rot-resistant chestnut, catalpa, black locust, red cedar, or Osage orange. "My great-grandfather had to replace all these fences in 1863," she said, beginning an old familiar story. "The soldiers camped here the night before the fight over in Gettysburg. They were supposed to take only the top rails of the fences to build their cooking fires. Of course when the top rail was removed, the next one down became the top rail and was fair game. He refused to use his good timber for rails, and built the fences with the crooked stuff that was no good for anything else. Some of those rails were so crooked that a horse could jump over the fence and still be inside."

Of course, there is more to managing a woodlot than thinning out the unproductive growth. Martha-Mac had to be careful about thinning too heavily. The added light could cause the remaining trees to sprout new branches, making knotty timber. Trees need to be cut when they are ready; otherwise they can go bad like "apples that hang too long on the tree." Leaning trees can develop nasty wood that torments anyone trying to plane it smooth. Most of Martha-Mac's work would take so long to have an effect that it would only benefit the grandchildren. Fortunately, thoughts of this had never stopped her grandfather.

The hill was covered with a rich woodland reflective of the energy that Martha-Mac put into the land. That was why the old beech trees on the top stood out. They were well past their prime, probably two hundred years old. Branches had broken from their tops, and one was completely hollow. Their bark was scarred and furrowed as high as a man could reach. "Why haven't you cut out these old beeches?" I asked. "Stand back and see if you can still read the date on the one in the middle," was her answer.

I squinted at the tree and realized that the scars were actually barely legible writing carved into the bark. I read the date slowly, "June 30, 1863." "The soldiers carved their names in these trees the night before the battle." She spoke quietly, as she pointed over toward Gettysburg. "When I was young, I could still read most of the names. These trees belong to them."

2

Building On

The carelesse waste . . . of our wonted plenty of timber, and other building stuffe, hath enforced the witt of this latter age to devise a new kind of compacting, uniting, coupling, framing, and building, with almost half the timber which was wont to be used, and far stronger.
– Robert Reyce, Suffolk, England, 1603

Bayleaf, a 15th-century timber-frame home preserved at the Weald and Downland Open Air Museum at Singleton, Sussex. This gets my vote as the most beautiful home on the planet.

THE CARPENTER

How can one person make a building that will endure for centuries when another's work falls apart and turns to compost long before its builder does? Take some time to study the skeleton of a well-framed old barn. (It must have been well framed—it's still standing, isn't it?) You will soon see the truth of what a 1745 book of trades said of the carpenter, that "strength is the chief of his study."

Study the frame, the vertical posts, the horizontal beams and diagonal braces. Older than Stonehenge, this "post-and-beam" construction is the essence of the English building tradition. Indeed, those first frightened English settlers in the New World built houses and barns that were not much different from the ancient stone monuments that they left behind: simple frames consisting of posts set into the ground, with beams spanning their tops. They were wooden houses, but hardly the work of carpenters. It's no wonder there aren't any of them left.

If you think of a building as a human body, then the carpenter's job is to make the bones and the skeleton—the strong frame to which the joiners and roofers will later apply the protective skin. Good carpentry makes strong frames by exploiting the strength of wood in three basic ways: in sizing the individual timbers of the building, in the connections between these pieces, and in the design of the frame as a whole. When all these aspects of the building are correct and working together, the carpenter has earned a good day's pay.

Beams

Take a wooden pencil and try to push it in from the ends to make it shorter. No go. Now bend it and it will snap in half. The point of this pencil exercise is to show that it is easy to make a strong post but harder to make a strong yet lightweight beam. You need a way to size your timbers so that they are stronger, but not heavier, than they need to be. Fortunately there is a simple guideline to help you to do this:

> The strength of a rectangular beam varies in direct proportion to changes in its width, but as the square of changes in its depth.

Imagine that you have to support a load with a beam measuring 2 inches wide and 4 inches deep. A 4 by 4, twice as wide, would be twice as heavy and twice as strong. A 2 by 8, however, twice as deep as the original timber, would also be twice as heavy but would have *four times the strength*. A 2 by 12 would be only three times as deep and heavy but nine times as strong. The more carpenters know about the strength of timbers, the more confidently they can approach the limits of the material.

In the eighteenth century, scientific testing attempted to remove some of the subjectivity from this question, but, as Oliver Wendell Holmes later observed in 1858, "Science is a first-rate piece of furniture for a man's upper chamber, if he has common sense on the ground floor." As a physician, Holmes well understood the difficulty of imposing mathematical predictability upon the messy organic world. His most familiar popular verse draws its humor from the problem of measuring and predicting the behavior of infinitely variable wood. The subject of his "logical story," "The Deacon's Masterpiece," was a carriage built with each part as strong as the others, with the result that it could never break down but only wear out. The Deacon, of course, started with first-class timber.

> So the Deacon inquired of the village folk
> Where he could find the strongest oak,
> That couldn't be split nor bent nor broke,—

And by using only the best wood, including ash "from the straightest trees," he constructed a carriage so sturdy that it ran for one hundred years to the day and then

> It went to pieces all at once,—
> All at once, and nothing first,—
> Just as bubbles do when they burst.

The Deacon's ideal creation is based on a fundamental quest of the builder. Joseph Moxon stated both the objective and the obstacle of this pursuit in his 1678 *Mechanick Exercises*. In his lessons on making the basic mortice-and-tenon joint, Moxon observed that "if one [the mortice or the tenon] be weaker than the other, the weakest will give way to the strongest when an equal Violence is offer'd to both. Therefore you may see a necessity of equalizing the strength of one to the other, as near as you can. But because no rule is extant to do it by, nor can (for many Considerations, I think,) be made, therefore this equalizing of strength must be referred to the Judgement of the Operator."

It's the old "a chain is only as strong as its weakest link" problem. But not even the limitless variability of wood could dampen the insufferable human drive to measure and quantify, although such wise nineteenth-century scientists as the great Peter Nicholson knew the limits of their scientific testing: "Yet it is impossible to account for knots, cross-grained wood, &c., such pieces being not so strong as those which have straight fibres; and if care be not taken in choosing timber for a building, so that the fibres be disposed in parallel straight lines, all rules which can be laid down will be useless."

One problem with strength tables is the changing nature of the material as the older, slow-grown timber is replaced by faster-grown, knottier, and coarser stuff. In 1786, the Carpenter's Company of Philadelphia tried to

[opposite]

Garland Wood pegs a pine brace to the oak sill of a blacksmith shop at Williamsburg. The mortice in the sill is open to one side and takes less time to cut than a more secure, fully housed mortice.

Robert Watson awaits the rest of the crew to help raise the walls of a reconstructed slave quarter at Carter's Grove Plantation.

address this problem in the only way they knew, by raising prices. Their "Rule Book" (a secret price-fixing manual) complained that "the stuff also used at this time is certainly from one sixth to one eighth more labour than that used some years ago, it being in general so much worse—and to expect work now, . . . for the same price by the square that the workmen had then, can hardly be deemed equitable or just."

To further complicate matters, the strength of a structure is determined by both the greenness of the wood and the greenness of the carpenter. Even the same piece of timber relentlessly changes in character from the moment when it is first cut down. An off-square saw cut on the base of a column can reduce its strength by 40 percent. One builder working on the College of William and Mary in 1704 was hauled into court because "partly by the Plank & timber being green and unseasoned & partly by employing a great number of unskilled workmen to complying his haste, [the building] was shamefully spoilt."

So you can look at tables to calculate the strength of timbers and joints. This information, coupled with a generous safety factor, should allow you to design structures that will meet the challenge of the centuries. But no table or formula can be trusted unless it is supplemented by an equally trustworthy and experienced eye for the quality of wood and workmanship. Oliver Wendell Holmes put it best. "Knowledge and timber shouldn't be much used till they are seasoned."

Joints

You will often hear that old buildings are held together entirely by wooden pegs. I well remember an early beer commercial that featured a sea gull

The walls are up, and Robert begins covering the frame with split-oak clapboards. The end brace of split oak is simply spiked in place.

The tower of Bruton Parish Church in Williamsburg, Virginia, built by Benjamin Powell in 1769.

[opposite]
The 1715 roof framing of Bruton Parish Church. The timbers are of tulip poplar cut from old-growth forest, a deep-green wood very unlike the white tulip poplar available today.

pulling a peg from an old house, causing it to totally collapse. Yes, the pegs are there, but the strength of these buildings is not in their pegs but in their joints. These mortice-and-tenon joints interlock the timbers so that they are solidly seated within one another. It is a rare older building from which you couldn't remove every peg and have it stand as strong as before. (Try this with the nails in a contemporary structure.)

Braced Frame

Although a post planted deeply in the ground won't fall over, this is hardly the best way to prevent destruction by termites and rot. Once you protect a building by placing it up on foundations, you must stiffen it by incorporating the immutable strength of triangles into the rectangular frames.

Diagonal braces work in several ways to strengthen the building. Ideally, a post is a perfectly vertical column that is under compression but not bending stress. If the post does start to bend, however, it can easily snap under its load. Braces connected to the post prevent such a bend from getting started. Braces also prevent the collapse of a building under wind load by blocking the closure of the right angles. The timbers must shatter or the joints break open before the building can begin to lean.

Braces are the most difficult part of a frame to cut and fit. I have seen people swear never to touch a chisel again from sheer frustration with fitting braces. Trimming one end of a brace makes the other end move in an arc. It must then be trimmed, which makes the first end move again. One building being framed by beginners had almost half as many braces left over, spoiled by bad cuts, as were finally used in the whole building. But both the building and the builders are stronger for the experience.

STEEPLE STORY

I sometimes dream of . . . a vast, rude, substantial, primitive hall, without ceiling or plastering, with bare rafters and purlins supporting a sort of lower heaven over one's head,—useful to keep off rain and snow, where the king and queen posts stand out to receive your homage.
– Henry David Thoreau, Walden, *1854*

Roof framing brings us literally to the pinnacle of the carpenter's trade. Seldom do we see in walls the skill, the challenge that we find in roof framing. A roof is strength and beauty combined, recognized in the 1734 *Builder's Dictionary* as "the most difficult and most useful Part of Carpenter's Work." In most towns of any age at all, you will discover a diversity of roof designs. Even within a single old building you can gauge the passage of the years by the technical changes in the framing of the roof.

Don't pull that peg! The queen posts of this truss are under tension and help support the long tie beam below them. A king post roof has but a single central post and works much the same way. This truss is part of the roof of the 1850 barn at Stagville Plantation near Durham, North Carolina.

Bruton Parish Church in Williamsburg, Virginia, was built in 1720, with the steeple added in 1769. Climbing the stairs to the gallery, you can pass through a little door into an upper world of magnificent and massive roof framing. Huge tulip poplar beams span the 36-foot breadth of the church. These simple beams support the ceiling framing through the stiffness of their enormous cross sections. Such simplicity is possible only when trees of surpassing strength and quality can be had.

The principle rafters of the church are equally massive and simple, joined by high, horizontal tie beams. If placed low enough on the rafter pair, the tie beam resists the outward thrust of the rafter feet through its tensile strength. Walter Rose, in his memoir of a country carpenter's life, tells the story of a farmer's two overweight sons who tired of having to step over a tie beam that crossed the loft of their barn. They decided to saw out a section of the offending beam to make a passageway. With the final stroke of the saw, the timber parted and the roof of their barn spread flat upon them, pushing the walls apart as it fell.

Not every complex roof needs to exploit tension. Even the magnificent hammer-beam roof is fundamentally a collection of shortened posts in compression. A hammer-beam roof could have all the pins pulled and tenons shorn, yet stand as strong as ever. But fool with a tension truss and watch out!

Just such a tensional roof was built down the street from Bruton Church in 1740. The brick building, a small but substantial store, is only 24 feet wide, yet its roof is supported by four queen post trusses set 12 feet apart. The roof makes a genuine statement of solidity, as the same store has been doing business under the same roof for 250 years.

Leaving the attic of the church, we head for one of those places you have always wanted to go—through the little door and up to the top of the steeple. Opening the door and climbing the stairs, we are drawn upward on ever steeper stairways, up ladders to the clock level, and finally up through the network of timbers to where the bell hangs and then to the very top of the octagonal spire. As you climb, the timbers darken, stained by the two centuries of pigeon guano and dust that have blown in on the cold wind seeping through the shingles.

The timbers are inscribed with chiseled Roman numerals and carved names. These names are not those of the builders, but of the sons of countless church rectors who climbed up here while their fathers tended to business down below. The carpenters left their work as their signature. Walter Rose, the country carpenter, recalled his father's lessons in pacing off the cuts with an "iron square" and his father's pride in pointing out complex hipped roofs in which "all the timber for it was sawn at the yard, each separate piece to the correct length and splay, without temporarily setting it up in position." Prefabrication at the carpenters' yard or "framing ground" meant that all the timbers had to be numbered so that they could be reassembled at the site. Sometimes that site was very far away.

A CONNECTICUT HOUSE FRAME ON A CARIBBEAN ISLAND

London 29th Febry 1764

To Mr. Joseph Trumble

Sir

I want a Frame for a House, & Lumber to Compleat that Frame, which I fancy may be had very well from Connecticut in New England & desire you to undertake to provide the same for me, on the Lowest Terms, they are to be had for these; & ship the same to me, to the Island of Granada, in the West Indies. . . . I must also desire You to procure some Two or three Carpenters & Joiners, who shall come out, with the Frame & Lumber, to the s^d Island of Granada, to sett up & finish the same. . . . Write to me at the Granades, . . . that I may know what Time I may expect the arrival of this Vessell at the above Port—I am Sir Your most Humb^le Servt

Dr. Wm Bryant

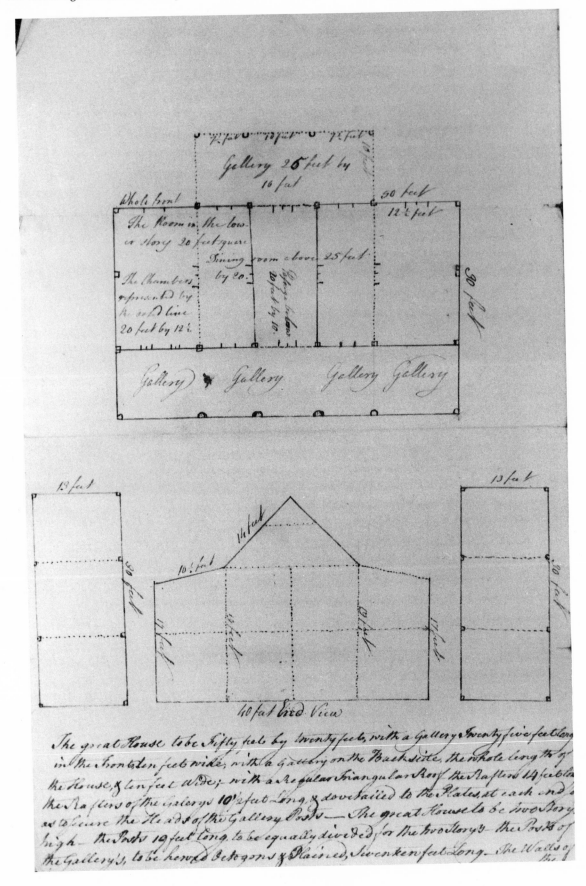

The great House to be Fifty feet by Twenty feet, with a Gallery Twenty five feet Long in the Front ten feet wide; with a Gallery on the Back side, the whole length of the House, & ten feet Wide; with a Regular Triangular Roof the Rafters 14 feet Long the Rafters of the Galerys 10½ feet Long, & dovetailed to the Plates, at each end as to secure the Heads of the Gallery Posts — The great House to be two Storys high — the Posts 19 feet Long, to be equally divided for the two Storys & the Posts of the Gallerys, to be hewed Octogons & Plained, Seventeen feet Long. The Walls of the

News of the letter from London traveled fast among the workmen of East Haddam, Connecticut. Work was always welcome in the riverfront town, and the prospect of sailing to the West Indies along with the doctor's house frame made for doubled excitement. The contract was no less welcome to Joseph Trumbull and his business partners. The years following the French and Indian War had not been good for them, and the opportunity to parlay their shipbuilding experience into a timber frame exporting business might save them from bankruptcy. If the contract with William Bryant was successfully executed, they might receive further commissions. The tropical island of Granada had been taken from the French only two years before, and there was talk of building a hospital and other government buildings there.

Joseph Trumbull wrote to his partners of the prospects for the workmen: "As for Joiners, to go to Granada . . . I think if they . . . are careful and prudent, it must be a good Jobb for them. . . . It will be best for one of them at least to Work in the Frames, that he may be the Better able to sett them up." The lead carpenter hired by the Trumbull firm was Isaac Fitch of Lebanon, Connecticut. Although he and his helpers built the house frame that summer, Fitch was not the one to go to Granada. He remained to build the New London County Courthouse and some of the finest homes in Connecticut.

The pine timbers and sweat for the proposed house came from Connecticut, but the design was by the London doctor and his West Indian wife. Specifications, along with a plan and elevation for the house, accompanied the letter commissioning its construction.

The great House to be Fifty feet by twenty feet with Galleries on the front and back. The great house to be two storys high—the Posts 19 feet long, to be equally divided for the two Storys—the Posts of the Gallery's to be hewed Octogons & Plained, Seventeen feet Long.

The Connecticut men may have found this an odd house frame to cut and fit, but the octagonal porch columns were easy work for men experienced in hewing shipmasts. The two-story-high porches on the front and back of the house would protect it from the tropical sun. The specifications also made clear where corners were to be cut and where they were to be beaded. "The Ground floor Timbers to be large & Strong & . . . hewed on one Side only," but "the Posts, Studds, Beams & Joists, that come in sight of the Chambers, to be plained, & a Bead run on the Edges."

The frame was soon ready and loaded aboard the brigantine *Olive*, which sailed from New London, Connecticut, in late July. The size of the ship made it "necessary to Splice the long Sticks of Lumber as they can't be Stowed on Board the Vessell." The bill for the house was recorded as paid by mid-October of that same year. Who would believe that a house could

[opposite]

The draft for the prefabricated house built in Connecticut in 1764 and shipped to the island of Grenada in the West Indies.

be ordered in England, framed in Connecticut, delivered two thousand miles away in the West Indies, completed, and paid for—all in the space of seven months?

But this feat was nothing new to carpenters of the old tradition. One or two skilled craftsmen could cut the joints in the timbers for houses, bridges, and windmills and only hire the big crew for the few days required to assemble and raise the frame on the site. The fact that the timber frame tradition is undergoing a great revival these days should come as no surprise. It is an ancient tradition with great strength behind it. The skills of the timber carpenter are adaptable to many tasks other than building construction. Carpenters may call upon their skill in shaping wood and their learned vocabulary of joints to make a variety of items. One common task of the carpenter is perhaps older and more widespread than building houses. Although a house can be made of stone or brick, the traditional hand-weaving loom can only be wood.

FOUR-HARNESS LOOM

These heavy looms, which have a great attraction, are also called barn looms, either because they ended up in the barn or because their framing looks like the frame of a barn. In fact, building this loom is really a small-scale timber framing job. When completed, it will take up about the same space as a baby grand piano. You can make it somewhat narrower, limiting the width of cloth that can be woven upon it. It does come apart, but that's no easy task.

The work begins with the timber. Seek out tight-grained stuff. Tight rings make hardwoods softer and softwoods harder. If you can get clear, old-growth hardwood, such as some soft white oak with the rings tight like a deck of cards, it will make a good loom. I am happy with clear, tight-grained yellow pine.

This loom is mostly framed of 4-inch by 6-inch timber. The wood will be a lot cheaper if you leave town to locate a small mill. The wood will probably be unseasoned, but you can get it dry enough in a few months just by keeping it inside. You will also need a couple of logs or big timbers to make the octagonal rollers for winding the warp (the long threads) and the woven cloth onto as the weaver works. You can also build up the timbers by gluing together smaller stock.

Tools

Aside from the usual measuring tools and a saw, you will need a mallet and a chisel stout enough to cut the big rectangular mortices through the posts. A big auger will help you with the holes, but you will still have a

An indoor timber-framing job—a four-harness weaving loom in the final stage of contruction at the shop.

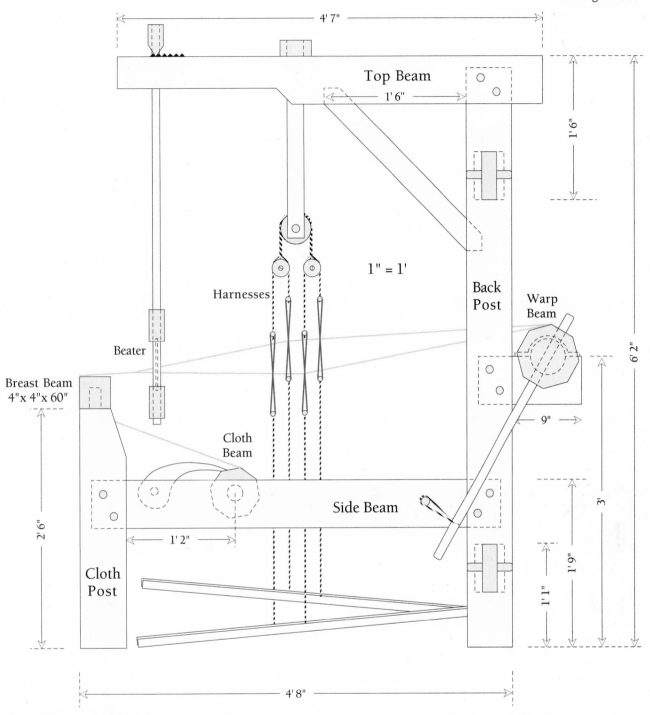

4' 7"

Top Beam

1' 6"

1' 6"

1" = 1'

Back
Post

Warp
Beam

Harnesses

6' 2"

Beater

Breast Beam
4"x 4"x 60"

9"

Cloth
Beam

3'

Side Beam

1' 2"

1' 9"

2' 6"

Cloth
Post

1' 1"

4' 8"

49 lin. ft. 4x6   5   lin. ft. 4x4

Lay out the 45-degree shoulders on the brace tenons by holding the framing square so that equal numbers (in this case 4 inches) intersect the edge on both the blade and the tongue.

tough time if your chisel is too small. You will need a gouge to carve the hollows that will support the bearings of the big beams. You will need a plane to finish and dimension the timbers and an axe or adz to rough out the big octagonal rollers. Octagons will do for all the rollers except where they bear at the ends, so you don't need a lathe.

The two sides of the loom are identical frames, so their components may be laid out in pairs. If this were a house or barn, they would be called "bents." They are joined with pegged mortice-and-tenon joints. Connecting the two side frames are three beams. These beams have long tenons on either end that extend through mortices in the frames. The tenons are themselves morticed where they stick out, making spaces for the keys that hold the loom together—until you want to knock it apart. Make the side frames first, then the crossbeams and rollers, then fit the remaining pieces.

Side Frames

Each side frame has three big joints and two smaller ones for the diagonal brace. It matters not which joint you cut first, but all must be carefully cut to keep the frame solid, square, and lying in the same plane. Big, ugly timbers require constant attention in order to keep the frame flat. Short of eyeballing the joints into a perfect whole, (which you can do) you will need to bring the area around each joint into the same plane on any given

The 1½-inch-wide tongue of the square
can also help you lay out the width of the
mortice.

timber. Consider a back post that connects with six other timbers. You can go all the way and true the entire timber (not such a bad idea), but it is only where the joints go that really matters.

One way to position the joints is by laying out snaplines, as in hewing timbers (in chapter 1), and then hewing only the areas around the joints down to the lines. Sufficient accuracy is possible only if you use long, straight sticks to magnify the errors of alignment. Set the faces in question upward and set perfectly straight sticks (at least 2 feet long—framing squares will do) where each joint will go. Get down and eyeball the sticks to see what corrections are necessary. By cutting and testing, all critical faces may be brought into the same plane. The intervening areas may be as rough as a cob, but the joints will spring from perfectly aligned planes.

Joint Layout

I usually prefer to lay out the joints in timbers of this size with a framing square. I use the square to locate the joint back from and parallel to the edge of the timber. A morticing gauge with its two teeth will sometimes lead you astray, as the fence rides over only the local area. The longer blade of the square averages out any errors, and, because it measures 1½ inches wide, it locates the tenon about as far from the edge as it needs to be. Scratch the first line and then move the square over so that the width of the square provides the width of mortice or tenon. In a 4-inch-thick timber, this method makes one cheek of the mortice a half-inch thinner (therefore weaker) than the other. A double-toothed morticing gauge set to mark equal cheeks would make a somewhat stronger joint, but this is a good way to work when you need speed and accuracy with rough timber.

Tenons are easy enough to saw; it's just work. Cut them first, leaving them a little fat so that they can be trimmed later if need be. If your timber is greener than you thought, cutting the tenons first will give them a chance to dry and shrink before you trim them to final size. Bore your holes for the mortices with your auger and then square them with your chisel. Fit the first timbers together and leave them together as you fit the next set. Trim and pare the tenon of the second joint to bring the beams into alignment. You could adjust the mortices, but the tenons are easier to reach. Should a tenon shoulder fit flush on one side but stand off on the other, you may bring them both up tight by kerfing in the shoulders with your saw.

Once you have joined the top rail and back post to your satisfaction, lay out the joints for the brace before you knock it apart for pegging. Just lay the brace piece in position atop the assembled timbers and mark each piece where it crosses another. Bring the lines down and around the timbers with the square and cut the joints accordingly. Trial-fit your frame and make ready to drawbore.

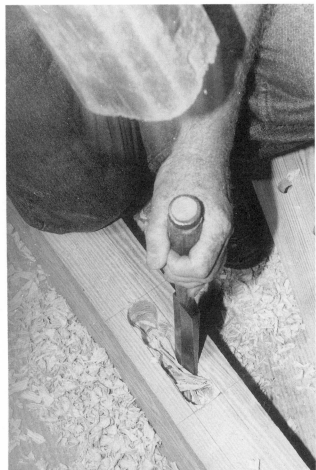

Drawboring

If you are making this loom for someone that you particularly like, you may gain an enhanced appreciation of your efforts by arranging for that person to be around for the drawboring and pegging of the frame. This tightening of a joint by deliberately offsetting the holes through the mortice and tenon is fun to do. This is a good time to share the work. Anybody can bore a hole or shave a peg, and this method of tightening a joint by deliberately offsetting the peg holes is a neat concept for people to discover.

With all of the timbers disassembled, bore the ¾-inch peg holes through the cheeks of the mortices. Drive one of the tenons home and mark the location of the auger hole through the cheek either by pushing in with the auger or by poking around with the scratch awl. Now pull the joint apart and bore the hole through the tenon, offset about ⅛ inch toward the shoulder of the tenon. Reassemble the joint and drive through a long, tapered peg to pull the joint up tight as a tick.

Just take care to offset the peg hole in the right direction, toward the shoulder of the tenon. Slackboring is hard to correct.

[left]

A large auger can make short work of most of the wood in the mortice.

[right]

Clean out the rest of the waste with a mallet and chisel.

Drawboring. Because the hole through the tenon is offset from those through the cheeks of the mortice, driving in the tapered peg forces the joint tighter and tighter.

Crossbeams

The beams that connect the two side ·frames are pretty straightforward. They need to be easily removable so that the loom can be taken apart. The upper back beam may be a 2 by 6. The tenons extend straight through the side frames and their peg holes are also offset toward the shoulders of the tenon. Leave the tenons plenty long, lest their ends shear off under the force of the tapered peg. These keyed tenons are drawbored in their own way, with the opening made deeper rather than flush with the surface through which they extend. This enables the wedging to force the joint tighter and tighter. The breast beam that the cloth wraps around sits on tenons atop the front posts. It must be a tight, smooth piece of timber to prevent snags as the woven cloth travels around it onto the cloth beam. These beams complete the frame and give you something to show for your work.

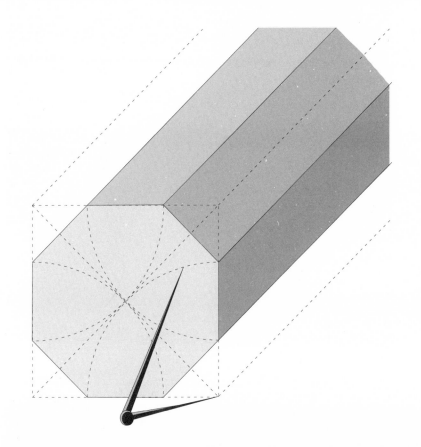

Laying out the octagon for the beams with four sweeps of the dividers, which are set to half the length of the diagonal of the original square timber.

Be sure to snap the lines for the octagon by straining the string in the same plane that you are defining. Any other angle will cause inaccurate lines.

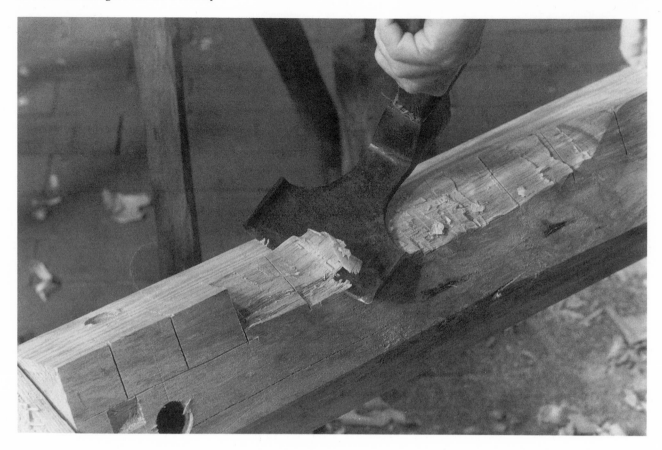

Saw cuts across the grain at regular intervals will ease the work of hewing and prevent a split from diving too deep.

Cloth and Warp Beams

The long threads need to roll off of one big, octagonal roller onto another big, octagonal roller. If you use a log, you may find that it's easier to square it with an axe before trying to make it octagonal. Once you have a timber squared, it's easy to lay out an octagon. Make sure the ends are square, then draw two diagonal lines on the ends connecting the corners. Set your dividers or gauge to equal the distance from the corner to the intersection of the two diagonals (the center of the timber). If you are using dividers, pace over from each of the corners onto the two adjoining faces. This will give you eight points on either end of the timber that you can connect with snaplines to guide your axework. If you use a gauge, run it down the length of the four corners of the timber, scratching onto the faces to make the equivalent lines. If the grain on your timbers is a little wild, make a lot of saw cuts down to these lines before roughing in the faces. Finish the faces with a plane and take a break.

Although octagonal cross sections will do for the parts of these beams around which the cloth wraps, the ends that bear as gudgeons to allow them to turn must be well rounded. Set your dividers in the center of the diagonals left on the ends and trace the size of the bearing gudgeon. Measure the distance from one face of the octagon to the outside of this circle to determine how deep you will need to cut. Stick a piece of tape on the

side of your saw to guide the depth of this cut and saw in all around the shoulders of the gudgeons. Chisel out the wood and rasp it smooth.

Now these gudgeons need a hollow place to bear upon. The heavy warp beam sits in hollows cut into the tops of short studs extending from the back post. Use the compass and square to trace half circles on both the front and back of the block. Make a series of closely spaced saw cuts down to the bottom of the half circle and chisel out the rough waste. Finish the hollow out to the line with a gouge and check for a smooth fit with the gudgeon of the roller. The cloth beam rides in holes bored into the inner faces of the side beams. A 1½-inch auger will make these holes in an instant. You can also make the holes with an expansion bit or, carefully, with a gouge.

Both the warp beam and the cloth beam need to be bored for crank holes. A hole should pass through each face of the octagon, allowing a lever to be inserted for turning the roller and, in the case of the warp roller, for holding it in a locked position. It is best to bore all of these holes in from the outside and aim to meet in the middle. You can do it. The cloth beam also needs to have some ratchet teeth chiseled into the faces of the octagon to catch the end of the pawl as it pivots off the inner face of the right front post.

[left]

Cutting the round bearing surfaces or gudgeons on the beams. Split away the bulk of the wood after making saw cuts to a measured depth around the circumference of the octagon.

[right]

Saw cuts also make for safer work in roughing in the pillow blocks that hold the warp beam.

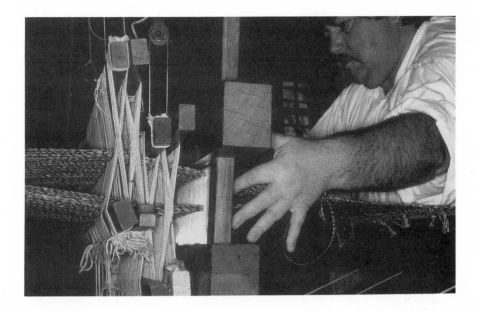

Harness

So far, we have made only the frame of the loom that holds the long threads. In this next part we will construct the foot-operated mechanism that raises and lowers alternate groups of these threads to allow the insertion of the cross threads or weft. The long threads are divided among four harnesses and ride up and down with them, opening up spaces for the weft to pass through. A four-harness or four-shaft loom uses three rollers. One roller suspends two smaller rollers, which suspend two harnesses each. The harnesses ride up and down on either side of these pulleys, giving rise to the name counter-balance loom. The rollers can be turned on a lathe or built of octagons, as with the cloth and warp beams.

The main roller hangs suspended in a frame, in the same manner as the cloth beam. Mortice and tenon and peg this frame together, and the roller can be sprung into place. The main roller should be about 4 inches in diameter and should turn on 1-inch-diameter gudgeons.

The secondary rollers can be a bit more than an inch in diameter. They, too, can be octagonal or round. If you turn them on the lathe, you can make the suspension bearings at the same time. Before you remove the roller from the lathe, turn a groove for the suspension cord about a quarter-inch in from each end. Then turn in a parting cut about a quarter-inch beyond that, but don't cut all the way through. Take the roller from the lathe and drill a pilot hole into each end that extends past the parting cut. Now saw the end pieces off and enlarge the pilot holes through them so that they will turn easily on the shaft of a round-headed screw long enough to reach into the pilot hole left in the end of the roller shaft. Hang the rollers on sash cord so that they will be in a straight line from the warp beam to the breast beam, but wait until the heddles are in place before tying them permanently.

Weaver Max Hamrick on his loom at the Wythe House in Williamsburg. The four harnesses carry the hundreds of string heddles that control the threads. The heavy oak beater swings from above and carries the reed that packs the weft into the warp.

[opposite]
Bore holes through the cloth beam to take the winding lever, and chisel ratchet teeth to engage the pawl. Winding this beam takes up the woven cloth and keeps the threads under constant tension.

This pine beater carries the reed within grooves plowed into the upper and lower cross members.

Shafts, Heddles, and Treadles, but No Lams

Suspended from the secondary rollers are the four shafts or harnesses. These are nothing more than round sticks with heddles hanging from them. A heddle is a loop of string with an eye tied in its middle. The weaver will need hundreds of these, because each one controls the position of one long thread that passes through its eye. The lower ends of each set of heddles are also speared by a shaft that is in turn connected to the foot treadles. These treadles pivot from an anchor attached to either the back of the loom or to the floor.

You may get some questions here about things called lams. These are intermediate levers that allow you to use six treadles to more easily control the four harnesses in a greater number of ways. They are just four small levers that pivot off of the side beam. Let the weaver who wants them show you where they should go. The weaver should tie the heddles, too, and he or she should order (or make, for someone who is really into it) the reed, the final part for this loom.

Beater

The beater swings from the top beams and carries the reed that drives the weft threads into a tight weave as they are added. It is like a heavy comb on a swing; indeed, I discovered two children playing on the beater one day as if it were a porch swing. No harm done, but that's a lot of weight on the loom. The beater needs to have enough mass to hold the reed firmly and to provide some measure of inertia to the force of the beating. The hanging battens can be 1 by 3s, but the top and the two bottom pieces should be at least 2 by 3s. Make them from a 2 by 6 ripped down the middle. The three horizontal pieces are pierced by the two verticals, so lay out their mortices all at once. The vertical batten needs only some holes through it, judiciously spaced to allow for adjustment in the vertical plane. The two lower parts of the beater that house the reed need to have a half-inch-wide groove plowed down their length. If you do not possess a plow plane to cut this groove, you can do it quickly with a chisel. Do invest in a double-toothed morticing gauge with long, sharp teeth to score the surface of the wood on either side of the grove before you try this latter method. It's worth it.

If you put some kind of finish on the loom, be sure that it will not get onto the threads and make the finished cloth smell like linseed oil. If you have used righteous wood, it will need no finish. Setting up a loom for weaving is a job almost equal to making the loom to begin with, but this is, of course, a job for the weaver.

Unlike carpenters, weavers are among the elect that must sit at their work. Perhaps this is why Shakespeare gave the name "Bottom" to the weaver among the "rude mechanics" rehearsing the play-within-a-play in *A Midsummer Night's Dream*. Shakespeare, as we shall see, was not above weaving a few digs at his fellow craftsmen (for he was but a play*wright*) into his contributions to the "wooden O."

Frank Grimsley planing the stock for
doors and windows.

THE JOINER

This fellow will but join you together as they join wainscote; then one of you shall prove a shrunk panel and, like green timber, warp, warp.
– William Shakespeare, As You Like It, 1598

Shakespeare wrote these lines comparing a sham wedding to shoddy joinery exactly one year after he bought his new house in Stratford-on-Avon from an ancestor, William Underhill. It's comforting to know that your family work can serve as an inspiration to others.

A century later Joseph Moxon, in his book *Mechanick Exercises*, offered a definition of joinery as it should be: "JOINERY, is an Art Manual, whereby several Pieces of Wood are so fitted and join'd together that they shall seem one intire Piece." This is much the same as a carpenter's work but for the fact that "Joiners work more curiously, and observe the Rules more exactly than Carpenters need do."

Long before the carpenters completed the framing of Shakespeare's house, the joiners would have been at work making his doors and windows, staircases, and trim. Quite likely their work was not even undertaken at the construction site but rather at their joiners' shop in the village. Here they could keep their glue pots and wood, their saws and mallets and chisels, and, most significant, their planes and benches.

Planes and benches mark the beginning of the joiner's territory. They go together like carpenters and beer. When woodworking planes were first developed during the Roman era, they created the need for a long, level surface to support the work at a convenient height. For the joiner of average stature, that height is about 30 inches. This elevation is ideal for planing and for the light chisel-and-saw work of joinery, but it is too high for heavy carpentry and too low for carving and fancy work.

Even if he doesn't create fancy mouldings, the joiner needs a lot of planes. Just as the speeds on a bicycle match the rider's strength to varying terrains, the key to a joiner's efficiency is the use of a tool that is precisely suited to each stage of the work. The joiner's planes make progressively finer and broader cuts as the work progresses. Trying to bring rough stock to precise dimensions with a single plane is like riding a one-speed bike in a hilly town.

Starting off with a relatively short scrub or jack plane that has its iron (as the blade is called) ground to a convex profile, the joiner can quickly level the surface of the wood. The parallel hollows left by this initial step can then be smoothed out by the finer-cutting trying plane; the final, dead-level surface is rendered by the jointer. The long jointer plane uses its great length (around 30 inches) to keep the iron from cutting wood in the valleys until the hills are all shaved down. When the shavings emerge from the plane unbroken for the entire length of the stock being planed, the

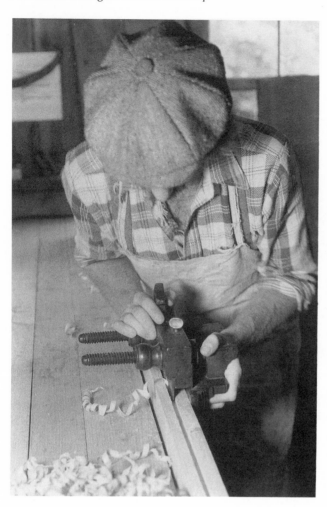

[left]

This 1870 plow plane has adjustable screw arms that position the cutting blade at any distance from the edge of the timber. An assortment of blades or "irons" allows for different widths of grooves, and a thumbscrew-adjusted stop controls the depth. The plow plane is an essential tool of the joiner.

[right]

Garland Wood finishes off one of the great panel-frame doors for the restored courthouse in Williamsburg. Because the inset panels are free to swell and shrink within grooves plowed in the frame, the outer dimensions of the door will remain stable regardless of the humidity.

surface must be level and true (or close to it). It is an occasional tradition in some shops to tack the longest unbroken shaving on the wall over the bench. Our current ribbon of pine runs 27 feet, 3 inches.

One other specialized plane that the joiner needs is the plow. The adjustable plow cuts a groove into the wood a given distance from one of the edges. By making a rectangular framework from this grooved stock, the joiner can slip broad panels into the spaces to cover as large an area as necessary. This is panel frame construction, a fundamental task of the joiner, most often seen in the classic panel door and in Shakespeare's wainscot.

The problems with Shakespeare's wainscot, the shrinking and warping, stem both from the nature of wood and from human nature. The purpose of panel frame construction is to allow the inevitable shrinking and swelling of the broad panels to take place harmlessly within the grooves cut for them in the frame. Only when the work is done hastily, with unseasoned stock, will the shrinkage be so great that the panels will pull free of the grooves and "warp, warp." The seasoning of the material is so important that it is common practice to make doors in stages, allowing for "second seasoning." The joiner will bring the material almost to its final size, then set it aside for about a week before continuing. Oak is particularly prone to shrinkage after a fresh surface is exposed. The *Builder's Dictionary* warned of this: "For it has been observ'd, that though Boards have lain in an House ever so long, and are ever so dry, yet when they are thus shot and planed, they will shrink afterwards beyond Belief."

George Eliot's 1896 novel *Adam Bede* begins in a joiners' shop, where a distracted young worker calls out, "There! I've finished my door to-day, anyhow." To his embarrassment, and to his coworkers' amusement, he is holding up an empty frame for approval, having forgotten to make and fit the panels. Like the joiner who forgot the panels, we forget how the design of the panel frame door has evolved directly from the behavior of wood and water.

The idea for framed work is ancient. Frame carpentry began with simple skeletal structures of timber, the spaces between filled in with interwoven sticks plastered over with clay. When this design is extended to joinery, it perfectly solves the problem of wood and water. Although wood shrinks and swells across the grain, it is remarkably stable along its length. When the framing of a door—or wainscot—is constructed with the long grain of the wood, its outer perimeter will not swell or shrink. The broad panels within this stable outer frame can then expand and contract within the grooves cut for them. The result is a door that does its job; it opens and closes at your command, never sticking or cracking with the weather.

For this strategy to work, of course, the wood panels must be free to move. Even today, workers who do not understand the fundamental principle of panel frame construction doom their door to failure by overuse of the glue pot. The *Builder's Dictionary* warned joiners to leave the panels free of glue and nails, for "This will give Liberty to the Board to shrink, and swell without tearing; wheras Mouldings that are nailed round the Edge, as the common Way is, do so restrain the Motion of the Wood, that it cannot shrink without tearing;"

In the days of the village joiner's shop, making a basic, four-panel door was considered a good day's work. This meant ripping, planing, and grooving the stiles and rails of the frame, laying out and cutting the ten mortice-and-tenon joints, planing and molding the four panels to fit into the grooves of the frame, and then fitting the whole together. This job admits not the slightest carelessness. As Peter Nicholson's 1860 *Dictionary of Architecture* cautioned, both the tools and the workman must be sharp and true, "these being strictly attended to, the work will of necessity, when put together, close with certainty; but if otherwise, the workman must expect a great deal of trouble."

Shakespeare may not have been entirely displeased with the work of his local joiners. One of the other "rude mechanics" in *A Midsummer Night's Dream* is a joiner who, although a dimwitted character, is at least given the name "Snug."

A great ogee cornice plane made for the crown moulding of the Williamsburg courthouse. The plane's tow rope allows several people to help remove the 7-inch-wide shaving from the hard yellow pine.

[opposite]

Cutting in the throat in the pearwood block to make the cornice plane. The guidelines on the sides show the bed angle of the plane iron (45 degrees) and the angle for the tapered wedge above it.

MAKING PLANES

Sure, a plane may be just a block of wood with a piece of steel in it, but it is wood and steel so finely crafted that it strokes its order into all wood that it touches. This union of steel and wood poses an immediate problem. Wood changes its dimensions with changes in humidity; steel does not. If the wood that you choose for your plane is not dimensionally stable as well as hard and long-wearing, it will move out of tune with the steel. This is why your first job in plane making is to find a dimensionally stable wood, such as beech, birch, apple, boxwood, or pear, and put it aside for two or three years to dry and settle down. Cover the ends of the billets with wax to keep cracks from forming. Wood looses moisture through its end grain much faster than through its sides. When the ends dry faster than the middle, they also shrink faster. The fat, wet wood in the middle holds the wood on the ends apart, so the only way it can shrink is to crack into smaller pieces. Waxing the ends prevents this cracking by causing all the water to escape evenly out the sides.

You learn to make planes in the same way you learn to make anything from paintings to violins—by copying the works of past masters. If you

A series of holes made with small drills can be connected and lengthened by a keyhole saw.

copy a good plane and modify only the cutting face, you will learn to make planes for any job. Begin by squaring up the stock and laying out the throat lines on the sides. These lines will guide your chisel as you cut the opening for the blade or iron. The angle of this opening is usually a 45-degree pitch but may well be steeper for working harder wood. Make a pitch block, a board with the end cut at the required angle to guide your tools.

You can begin the opening by making holes with a long drill. (At Williamsburg we had to make a score of planes to use in reconstructing the mouldings during the restoration of the Courthouse, and we went through a half-dozen long bellhanger's gimlets starting the throat cuts.) Once you have a short row of holes through the body, the chiseling will go much faster. In larger planes, a keyhole saw can join the holes and make an even bigger space. Once you have an area for the chisel to reach into, the work is easy.

To keep cutting with the grain, you need to cut back from the bottom of the plane as you pare the upper surface of the throat. Rasps and coarse files will help you level the surfaces within the throat. Plane makers use coarse, single-cut files called floats to finish these inner spaces. You can make floats with a cold chisel and steel blanks, but a cabinetmaker's rasp will do as well, or you can do just fine with narrow chisels.

Scratch Stocks

Professional plane makers use planes to make their planes. These "mother planes" are fashioned so that their bottoms have the opposite shape from the pattern needed. Easy enough, but how do you get the mother plane? With a grandmother plane? No. You can use a scratch stock, a simple scraper blade mounted in a wooden block, which can make any moulding you need.

You can make the scratch stock for pennies and in just a few minutes. First, draw the moulding profile you need on paper and glue this pattern to an old handsaw blade. Cut off the piece of handsaw blade by scoring it deeply with a triangular file and snapping it off in the vise. Protect your eyes. File the blade down to the outline of the moulding pattern, making sure to file the edge square across. You can now use this scraper freehand or mount it in a block of wood and use it to smooth the gouged and planed contour. As with any scraper, use it only for the final precision shaping and smoothing after you have thoroughly roughed in the pattern that you're after.

The Blade

Once the throat and the bottom profile of your plane are complete, you can shape the cutting iron by insetting the blank and grinding it to match the profile of the bottom. If you are so fortunate as to have access to blacksmiths who can forge-weld laminated iron and steel blades, then we probably know a lot of the same people, because this is a rare skill indeed. But although early plane irons were laminated, you can do very well with solid tool steel forged or ground to a gentle taper to lock it against the pressure of the wood as it cuts.

Once you have the blank iron, you need to return to the woodworking and make the wedge to hold the iron. This is one of the most critical operations of plane making, for two reasons. First, the wedge must hold the iron tightly and securely to prevent chattering or slipping. You can seat the iron snugly against the wood by coating it with soot from a candle and then setting it in place so that it will leave marks on the high spots, showing you where to cut away. Second, the wedge and its socket must allow the shavings from the planing to pass freely out. The curvy shape of a moulding generates a shaving that is wider than the blade. Study the nuances of planes similar to the one you are making. There is a reason for every bevel in the wedge.

The plow allows you to accurately rough in the profile of the bottom in a series of steps.

Smooth the steps into the finished contour with gouges and other planes.

[opposite]

The bed of this little ogee plane was first roughed in with gouges and then finished with a scraper filed from an old saw blade. This works much faster than you might think. Mounting the scraper in a wooden handle makes it a scratch stock. (See the later section on making the butterfly table for more on scratch stocks.)

Now, with the iron secure, lay a scratch awl flat on the molded plane bottom and scratch the profile of the curves onto the iron. Sight down the bed of the plane to ensure that the scratching is reasonably accurate. Knock the iron free by rapping the top face of the plane. If you are going to use files rather than a grinder for this job, you will need to soften (anneal) the steel—if it is not already soft—by heating it red hot and allowing it to cool slowly in the ashes. Once you have filed the blade to the proper profile, it will need to be rehardened by heating it red hot and cooling it rapidly. Temper the blade by reheating it once more until the edge shows an oxidation color of bronze heading toward a tinge of purple and then quickly cooling it again. Hone it to the final cutting edge using curved slipstones.

As you use your new plane, you will discover soft or brittle places in the blade and chattering or choking with the shavings. Overcoming these problems by resharpening and careful trimming is like tuning and adjusting the bridge on a new violin.

This section has provided only a short treatment of a complex undertaking, so I direct you to the writings in the appendix if you wish to learn more from other books. The old planes themselves are equally accessible, and as teachers they are equal to ink.

William Buckland, master joiner of the Chesapeake, in a 1789 portrait by Charles Willson Peale.

AN "UNKNOWN YOUNG MAN"

In 1925 a portrait of an "unknown young man painted by C. W. Peale" went on the auction block. The anonymous subject of the painting looked out confidently from the canvas. On the table beside him lay drawing instruments and the plan of a house. Behind him stood a classical portico and scaffolding. No one knew at the time that this "unknown young man" was responsible for some of the most beautiful homes ever built in America. No one knew William Buckland.

Buckland's story emerged slowly in this century. In the original 1929 White Pine monograph series on the Hammond-Harwood house of Annapolis, Maryland, he was mistakenly identified as *Matthew* Buckland from Philadelphia. His work at Gunston Hall was attributed to "convict craftsmen from England" and to the "importation of the finished product from

England." Now scholars have pieced together the true story of Buckland's career as a master craftsman of the colonial Chesapeake. Architectural historians have identified the work of individual carvers in his employ and are gradually retrieving his creations from the insults of the centuries.

George Mason, the "father of the Bill of Rights," brought William Buckland to America in 1755. As was the custom of his class, Mason followed the advice of William Fitzhugh to "get a Carpenter, & Bricklayer Servants, & send them in here to serve 4 or 5 years, in which time of their service, they might reasonably build a substantial good house." While Mason began the simple brick exterior of Gunston Hall overlooking the Potomac, his younger brother Thomson Mason, who was studying law in London, sought out a suitable joiner and carver. Thomson found Buckland, who was then twenty-one years old and had just completed his apprenticeship. Thomson engaged him as an indentured servant to serve for four years in America.

The young Buckland was eager to show his skill. Gunston Hall soon became a catalog of the latest London styles. William Buckland had learned his trade as an apprentice to his uncle, a London woodcarver, joiner, and publisher of architectural books. Buckland owned fifteen of these books at the time of his death. The Chinese-style dining room in Gunston Hall was derived from one of them, Thomas Chippendale's *Gentleman and Cabinetmaker's Director*. This room is the first known chinoiserie in colonial America. The double-ring fretwork over the doors in the Palladian Room recalls that shown in Batty Langley's *City and Country Builder's and Workman's Treasury of Designs*. The southern-facing, garden porch was inspired by another Langley book, *Gothic Architecture*, and is the first expression of the Gothic revival in America. These were not only firsts, they were magnificent firsts.

But time takes its toll. A servants' stair, probably built at Buckland's suggestion, was removed. Mouldings were taken from the fireplace to use

The Gothic garden front porch at Gunston Hall, designed by William Buckland.

on doorways. Other alterations were made over the years, including the 1950 restoration by Fiske Kimball.

In 1982 architectural detectives began exploring at Gunston Hall. Charles Phillips and Paul Buchanan traced wear patterns, exposed ghostly paint ridges, and probed countless nail holes. They found that the original house was much more elaborately ornamented than anyone had imagined. Decorative carvings had been everywhere, even on the window muntins. The entrance hall had had twelve more pilasters, an elaborate frieze, and a false door. These have now been replaced, and work is underway on the other rooms. Slowly the house is returning to Buckland's design.

Buckland finished his indenture to Mason in 1759. Although technically a servant, he was highly respected and treated more like a member of the family. He left with George Mason's recommendation: "During the time he lived with me he had the entire Direction of the Carpenters and Joiners work of a large House; and having behaved very faithfully in my service, I can with great justice recommend him as an honest sober diligent man & I think a complete Master of the Carpenter's and Joiner's business both in theory and practice."

Buckland moved to Richmond County, Virginia, and began to diversify his skills in order to undertake larger projects. He worked for John Tayloe II at Mt. Airy (where only fragments of his distinctive woodwork survive) and at Sabine Hall for Landon Carter. He worked on Montpellier. He married, began a family, and once in 1764 (gentleman though he was becoming), was fined ten shillings for profane swearing.

The booming city of Annapolis soon called the former London apprentice away from country mansions. There he continued to be in great demand, decorating the senate chamber of the Maryland State House and finishing the Chase-Lloyd house. He had the job of "undertaker" on the Chase-Lloyd house in 1771–72, supervising the brickwork, shingling, and coarser stuff. In 1773 he was replaced as the undertaker and continued to work only on the delicate carving. He may have been preoccupied with thoughts of the lot across the street, where he was soon to build his masterwork.

Buckland began the Hammond-Harwood house in early 1774. Charles Willson Peale began his portrait of the confident young man with a plan at his side that same year. The house was of a mature design both inside and out, with superb details and some of the finest carving to be found anywhere. But Buckland was to see neither house nor portrait completed. The forty-year-old William Buckland was dead by December. Perhaps his partner and former apprentice, John Randall, finished the house. Both Buckland's portrait and his work began to gather dust.

As with most of Buckland's surviving works, the Hammond-Harwood house has been preserved as a museum. You can follow Buckland's work

[opposite]
A collapsing ladder modeled after the one in the library at Gunston Hall.

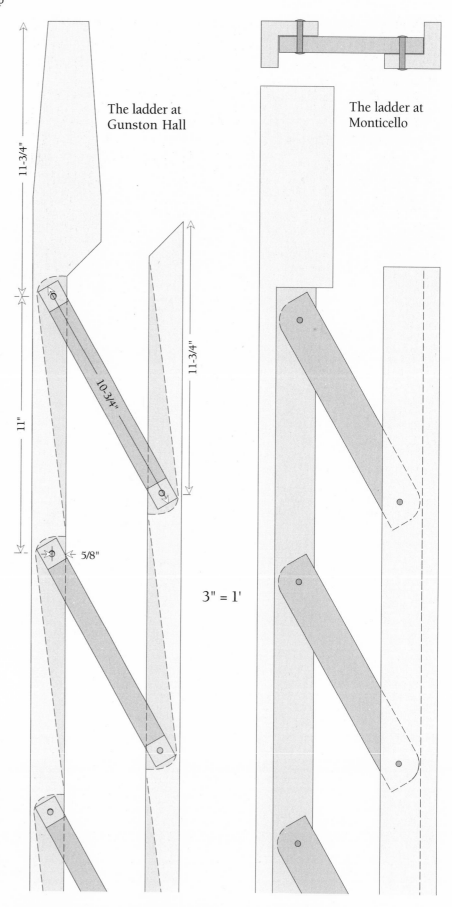

The ladder at
Gunston Hall

The ladder at
Monticello

3" = 1'

*The ladder at Monticello was modeled
after one that Thomas Jefferson saw on a
trip to Europe. On his return to Virginia,
he had a copy made from local wood. Its
angular cross section is much easier to
make than the round one of the ladder at
Gunston Hall.*

on a trail leading through Virginia and Maryland. Begin with the exuberant Gunston Hall, and finish your pilgrimage on the porch of the Chase-Lloyd house, from where you can look across the street to the final masterwork of William Buckland.

Drill the holes for the pivot pins through the first rung and use that as a guide to drill all the rest.

JEFFERSON'S LADDER

And he dreamed, and behold a ladder set up on the earth.
– Genesis 28:12

Leaning against the wall in one corner of the library at Gunston Hall is what appears to be a large pole. But bounce it lightly on the floor and it opens into a ladder that allows you to reach the books on the upper-most shelf. This design has a dubious attribution to Thomas Jefferson. It is quite an attention getter. I once took a copy of this collapsing ladder to a demonstration of pit sawing at a timber-building conference. I picked

up the folding ladder, bounced it open, and leaned it against the log atop the trestles. If I had hoped to interest anyone in the sawing, it was all over now. We sawed our hearts out, but the only thing people were interested in was the collapsing ladder.

A threaded pipe junction on a stick will help you smooth the interior of the rung hollows.

Rungs

Use your best wood for making these ladders. One side of each rung is supported solely by the pivot pin, and should this split under a heavy load, down you go. You can make the rungs entirely of wood if you understand the risks and choose your wood very carefully. (Remember that oak, hickory, and ash are strongest when the rings are wider.) You will do better to cap the ends with ferrules (collars) made from 1-inch-diameter, thin-walled brass pipe. Turn down a shoulder on the ends of each rung to make

[opposite]
Chisel out the rung hollows after boring holes at the deepest point of each.

Peen the ends of the pivot pins over washers and smooth the outside into a round or octagonal shape.

the collars fit flush with the wood. If you do not have a lathe, you can still fit the brass caps with a rasp or a chisel—it just takes a little longer. Indeed, if you don't have a lathe, there is no reason why you can't make the ladder with square or octagonal rungs.

This ladder is a geometrical construct that requires some precision to allow it to fold and unfold properly. Only a true parallelogram will fold completely flat. The rungs must all be of equal lengths and equally spaced. One short rung will cause the whole affair to snag.

Drill the holes for the pivot pins at one end only of all of the rungs first, measuring in ½ inch from one end. This done, drill the second hole in one rung as accurately as possible, straight and true. This will be the "master rung" and will guide the placement of all the holes in the rungs to follow. Set the master rung atop one of the single-hole rungs and place a length of ¼-inch rod through the first set of holes. Use the second hole in the master rung as a guide to drill the second hole through the lower rung. If you are careful not to enlarge the hole in the master rung as you continue, all of the pairs of holes in the other rungs will be exactly like this first one.

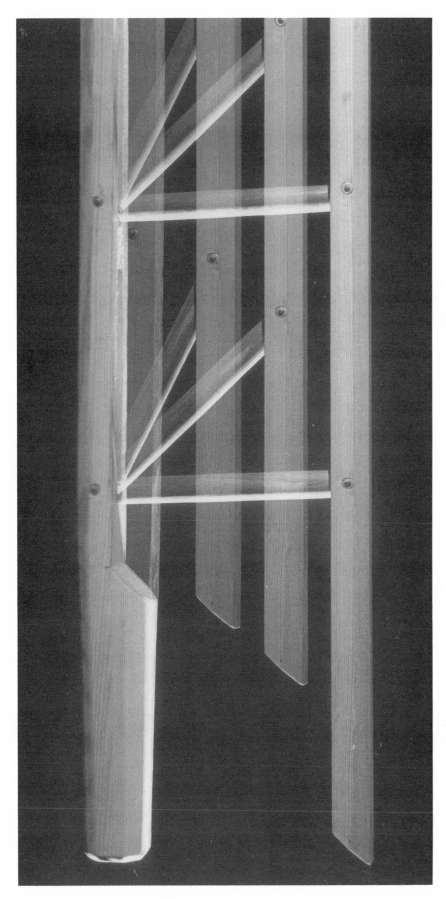

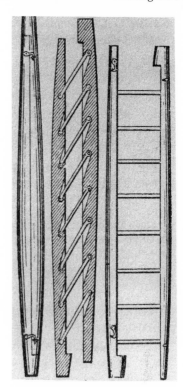

A similar collapsing ladder as illustrated in Knight's Mechanical Dictionary *of 1876.*

If all the dimensions are consistent, the ladder will fold easily as a perfect parallelogram.

Rung Hollows

When you have completed the rungs, you can cut their housings—sloping hollows within the uprights. Lay out the uprights by pacing off 11-inch divisions with a pair of dividers. Draw square lines across the broad face through these points and down around the two sides. These lines will be the centers for the pivot pins as well as for the 1-inch-diameter auger holes that begin the hollows. Use a morticing gauge to lay out the inch width of the hollows down the center of the uprights. Check the measurements at least twice before you begin cutting and try some mock folding operations as well.

Wrap a band of tape around the auger bit 1⅛ inch back from the cutting lips to act as a depth indicator and bore the holes. Drill the pivot pin holes through from both sides. Start the sloping hollow by plowing a narrow groove with a long chisel. This initial trench from the surface to the depths of the auger hole will guide the rest of your chiseling and gouging. The job will be easy if the grain of your wood is true. Untrue grain is hell. A rasp made from a length of threaded iron pipe on an oak handle will serve you well to smooth and true the holes.

Undercut the auger hole with your gouge on the far side from the trenching to give clearance for the tip-ends of the rungs as they swing up. To see how much undercutting you will need, set a rung in place, push through its iron pivot pin, and try it out.

When you have everything ready to go together, put all the rungs and pins in place and check for proper folding action. The action shouldn't be too stiff. A bounce on the floor should open the ladder on the first try. Once you are satisfied, lay out the offsets for either end. Basically, the falling side takes some of the top of the other side with it. The best ladders are sawn from one piece of wood, but you will achieve most of the same effect by nailing and gluing the cutoff from one side onto the other. Saw the cut at a 45-degree angle to match the ascending arc of the separation. This is a mighty bad point in the operation to screw up, so mentally check three times before you cut. Saw the pins off about a 1/16 inch above the surface of the sides. You may wish to counterbore seats for the washers. Peen the ends over by rapid tapping with a light hammer. Chamfer the corners or round off the whole thing and paint. This a handy ladder for elopements.

THE BRICKMAKER'S HAND

We stand back, admiring Gunston Hall. The cool brick has endured fire, decay, and centuries of summer heat. But if you step close enough to touch the brick of these walls, somewhere, in one of the bricks, you will find a handprint. It may even be the smaller (yet equally work-hardened) hand-

Bill Weldon and the crew at Williamsburg making bricks. After mixing the clay by treading it on foot, he slams it into wooden molds at the molding table.

*As each mold is filled, off-bearers carry it
to the drying field, turn out the bricks,
and return the mold to the molder.*

Firing takes several days of constant attention, night and day.

print of a woman or child. Remember how these great homes began—with axes in the forest, with shovels in the clay.

A family made these bricks. Most brickmakers came to know their clay from a score of barefoot summers (and winters) helping the family work. Brickmaking in the eighteenth century remained as labor-intensive as it had been in the stories of the Old Testament. Every brick of the tens of thousands required for a building had to be handled at least seventeen times before the builders even touched it. Some of the handling was as simple as turning a partially dried brick up on its side, repeated for each of the thousands of bricks in the drying field. Thousands of the hands belonged to children, who were growing up learning the trade of their ancestors.

If it had the right clay in the right place, a clay bank might become a brickyard serving many customers. Often, though, a brick home would rise from its own cellar hole. Winter, not an idle time, was the season for exposing the clay to the working fingers of frost on cold nights. Through the winter, too, wood for firing the bricks needed to be cut. The bricks for a single fireplace and chimney could consume ten cords of wood before the hearth was ever laid.

Blending clay and water to the right consistency for molding into brick, called tempering, could be done with just hoes and shovels. At considerably greater investment, the brickmakers could use a "wheel pit," which was simply a wagonwheel mounted on an axle that pivoted on one end and was drawn in an endless circle by an ox or mule to work the clay. The effects of wagon traffic on the clay of colonial roads did not pass unnoticed.

When kept supplied with tempered clay, a good brickmaker could mold two thousand bricks a day. Selecting just the right amount of clay, the brickmaker rolled it and folded it into a loaf, then slammed it hard into the wooden mold to fill it all the way to the corners. When a mold was filled (a matter of seconds), the brickmaker scraped the excess clay off the top and flipped it up on its side, ready for the offbearers to take to the drying field. In the field, the off-bearer turned the shaped clay out onto the ground and returned with the empty mold for the brickmaker to refill, continuing the ancient cycle of their labor.

From the moment the freshly molded bricks hit the drying field, the brickmakers were at the mercy of the weather. Frost and sun could crack the bricks, or a rainstorm could melt weeks of work. But that was not all. If the bricks were set to dry on the bare ground, earthworms or ants

Centuries later, the handprints of the brickmaker's children remain visible in the tower of Bruton Parish Church.

emerging beneath one simply continued the extra three inches to the surface. Throughout the night, creatures left their tracks in the soft bricks. A raccoon might cause but a minor flaw; a stray cow was disaster.

After several days in the open air, the bricks were hard enough to stack into covered piles for building into the kiln. Rather than using a fixed kiln, into which they loaded the bricks, brickmakers often used a "clamp," a stack of brick arranged in such a way as to form its own kiln. First they built fire tunnels, or "eyes." When these were laid up, the remainder of the brick were stacked above, about a finger's-width apart. The outer walls had to be stacked tightly and plastered with earth to channel the fire in the eyes through to the top of the clamp.

The first few days of burning the clamp were a test of patience. The bricks still contained enough water that they would explode like popcorn if heated too fast. During those first days, white clouds of steam roiled out of the top of the clamp. When the steam disappeared and the smoke began to run clear, the pace picked up. The crew, already tired from tending the fires night and day, now had to feed it almost constantly to reach and maintain the 2000°F temperature necessary to transform soft clay into hard brick. Soon the fires in the eyes became so hot that a bolt of hickory tossed into it would burst into flames before it landed. The top would begin to glow deep red with tiny hellish jets of flame. After several days, the top of the clamp sank in the middle, the fired bricks shrinking more where the fire was hottest. The clamp continued to emit searing heat for days after both the fuel and the brickmakers were exhausted.

Once it was cool, the brickmakers would tear down the clamp and sort their work according to hardness and color. The outside bricks would never get hot enough to fully harden. These "samel" bricks could be used only where they were protected from the weather by harder common brick that had been placed deeper in the clamp. From around the eyes, where the flames played directly on the clay, the brickmakers pulled dark-glazed clinker brick. Builders could decoratively mix these with common bricks as they laid up a wall. But that was another trade, out of the hands of the brickmakers. Their work was over now, soon to begin again.

3
Machines

Through the door came the regular hum of a lathe. The princess timidly opened the door which moved noiselessly and easily. She paused at the entrance. The prince was working at the lathe and after glancing round continued his work.

– Leo Tolstoy, *War and Peace*, 1869

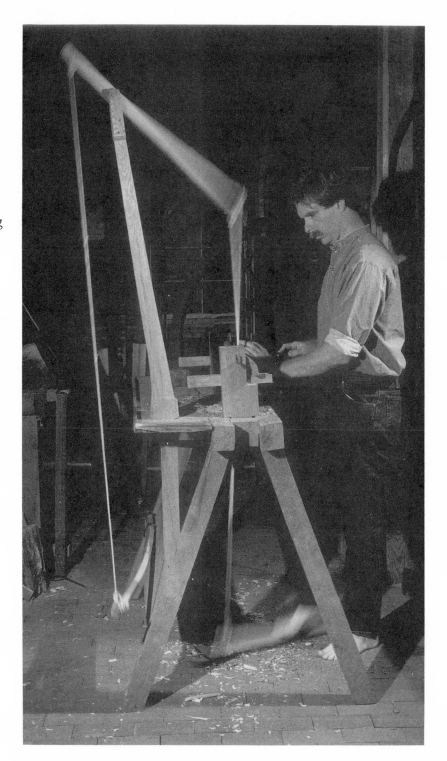

THE TURNER

If you were a wealthy aristocrat and could spend your time in any way you wanted, would anyone find you woodturning on a foot-treadle lathe? Perhaps not, but if you have done any woodturning at all, I'm sure you will agree that it is the most entrancing of all mechanical processes. The perfection of spinning symmetry revealed by the chisel holds a timeless fascination for prince and pauper as well. And if you really want to get back to basics, the Etruscan model of 1000 B.C. is hard to beat.

Your Basic Lathe Recipe

Take two stout posts with conical metal points (or even depressions) set in their sides. Bury the posts in the ground with the roughly rounded turning stock pinned between the two points. See that the wood spins freely but without any play from side to side. Now find a stout cord, a jug of cheap wine, and someone who doesn't look busy. Wrap the cord twice around the turning stock and give the two free ends to your assistant. Have that person pull alternately on the two ends of the cord to set the wood spinning back and forth. Shape the wood with your chisel as it spins toward you from the top. Use the wine to motivate the motion until the job is done.

Progress

Initial improvements to this lathe mainly involve means of keeping the *vino* to yourself. The cord can be stretched in a wooden bow to allow you to power the lathe with one hand, thus doing without the helper. This bow lathe is still used in many parts of the world. It leaves but one hand free to hold the chisel, but if you use your bare toes as a tool rest, you'll find that the work proceeds with astounding efficiency.

The Springpole Lathe

As useful as sit-down bow lathes are to the people of the Middle East, Europeans prefer to stand at their work (the better to see the boss coming). By attaching one end of the driving cord to a springy sapling pole and the other to a foot treadle, the turner can power the lathe on the downstroke and allow the springpole to pull it back when the foot is raised. The rotation still reverses on the upstroke, going about five full turns forward and five back, but such a lathe is powerful and fast, easily running up to 900 RPM. If designed with an adjustable bed that allows the points to adjust to different lengths of wood and an adjustable tool rest that accommodates different diameters, it is a versatile tool as well.

The turner using a classic springpole lathe. Before him are two common products of the turner's shop, a chair and a spinning wheel. This plate is from Van Vliet's 1635 Crafts and Trades.

The Great Wheel

Bow and springpole lathes work amazingly well when the mass to be turned is not large. But large heavy stock will have too much inertia to easily reverse direction on each cycle. The great wheel lathe solves this problem but brings back another. Simple but cumbersome, the 6-foot-diameter great wheel must be spun by a helper. A belt runs across the shop to the lathe bed, where it either wraps directly around the work or around a pulley on an iron axle, one end of which is spiked into the wood as a drive center. The great wheel lathe has the advantage of high speed and torque but again requires you to share the jug. When wind and water were judged to be cheaper sources of power than fermented beverage, the modern industrial era began. (Sigh.)

Folding Lathe

This folding lathe has consistently done well for me. It was designed by one M. Hulot of Paris in 1775. Although Hulot was primarily concerned with being able to fold it up and put it in a corner of the room, it is also an excellent lathe for traveling. It folds in the middle, and the legs can be pulled from their mortices and the whole thing packed up in a small bundle. I have found it to be not only a great attraction on market days but also a good working lathe. This is the first lathe I recommend to people who want to build their own.

This is, of course, a springpole lathe. The work, held between two conical points, spins as you pull down on a cord wrapped around it. The springpole rewinds the piece when you let up with your foot. Besides the fact that it folds up, the neat thing about this lathe is the compact mechanism of the springpole. Usually a springpole has to be about 12 feet long for there to be sufficient travel and spring to return the cord. This lathe, however, uses a short, stiff spring connected to the short end of a top-mounted lever. This gives the same action as a long pole, but in a very compact design.

The principles of construction are the same as for the loom, with the slight added complexity of laying out the mortices for angled legs. For a straight-in mortice, you can use the same setting on the double-toothed marking gauge for both the tenon and the mortice. When the tenon comes in at an angle however, the surface of the mortice becomes an oblique section, a diagonal wider than the tenon is thick. All this means is that after you lay out the tenons you need to readjust the gauge a little wider for the mortices. That's all.

The great wheel in a turner's shop, as illustrated in Hazen's 1846 Panorama, *a book of trades for parents and children. The man at the great wheel is powering a lathe that could also be run by a treadle at the turner's feet.*

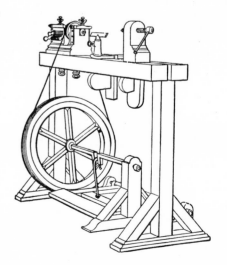

A treadle lathe from 1785.

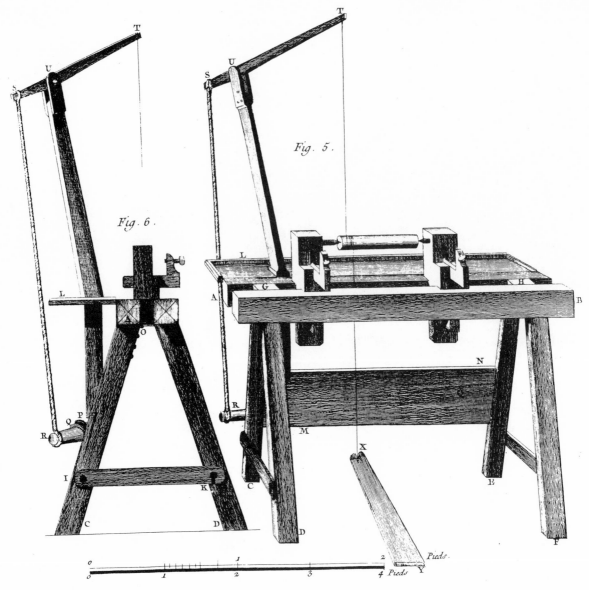

"It sometimes happens that devotees of woodturning are not well situated to have a permanently mounted lathe, or they may wish to work conveniently in a small apartment. For them, I have designed the bench in fig. 5, that may be folded and stored in a corner. A and B are two wooden side-beams of 3 to 4 inches square, connected together by two tie-beams, G and H, and standing on four wooden legs, C, D, E, and F. Two of these legs, D and F, are permanently mounted into the side-beam B, with mortice and tenon joints. The two others, C and E, are joined with double tenons to the long cross beam M, N, which is about 9 inches wide. These legs are moveable at the top, each having iron hinges which are attached with woodscrews on the inside as we see in O, fig. 6. The wooden cross beam I, K, is moveable at I, pivoting about an iron screw. The other end, K, catches by it's notch on a similar iron screw. One understands easily that this crossbeam holds the legs, C, D, at their proper spacing; and when one unhooks the crossbeam and folds it up along side of leg C, the leg may hinge at O, to fold up against leg D. The bench when folded occupies no more space than the thickness of legs C and D: the other end folds in the same manner at the same time. The shelf L, with its little rim around three sides, attaches to the side-beam, A, with little iron hinges. When one has removed the rocking arm pillar and the two poppets, one knocks over plank L and it will cover the two cross-beams A and B when one is not working. This plank L enlarges the bench and gives one a place to keep tools and work in progress"
—M. Hulot.

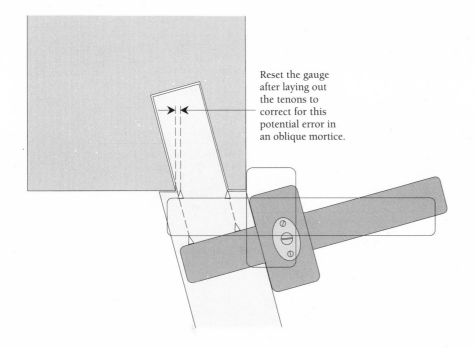

Reset the gauge after laying out the tenons to correct for this potential error in an oblique mortice.

THE WHEELWRIGHT

You need to readjust the morticing gauge when marking the opening of an oblique mortice.

You have already heard of the wonderful "one-hoss shay," the "Deacon's Masterpiece" of a carriage, which was built so well that it rolled for a "hundred years to a day" and then fell apart all in one great crash. The poem's author, Oliver Wendell Holmes, meant it only as a joke, but to a great extent the work illuminates the special nature of wheelwrighting. The wheelwright, perhaps more than any other woodworker, must know how to get the most from the wood. A wagonwheel must be light enough to move easily, yet able to carry tons of civilization over the rocks and ruts of the wilderness road.

Hubs

A wheel has no beginning except its center. The center is the hub, and for this the Deacon chose only the toughest stuff. "The hubs of logs from the Settler's ellum,"

> Last of its timber,—they couldn't sell 'em,
> Never an axe had seen their chips,
> And the wedges flew from between their lips,
> Their blunt ends frizzled like celery-tips;

The interlocked grain of elm enables it to be hollowed for the axle, pierced radially by a dozen mortices without splitting or cracking. The elm must be seasoned for seven years before it can be used—as long as it would take you to complete an apprenticeship in this trade.

The wheelwrights at Colonial Williamsburg. The men in the back are turning a new hub on the great wheel lathe.

Turning and Morticing

Much of your apprenticeship would likely be spent cranking the huge flywheel that powers the lathe used to turn the hubs from the seasoned elm. Each hub must be turned true to a cylinder so that it can be morticed to take the spokes. After pacing off their locations around the diameter of the cylinder with a pair of dividers, the wheelwright starts each of the mortices with a pair of auger holes. Wheelwrights are the primary users of the corner chisel, or "bruzz." The bruzz is L- or V-shaped in cross section and is essential for working elm; it cleanly severs the interlocked wood both along and across the grain. When the morticing is done, the hub goes back in the lathe and can be turned to the final shape of curves and seats for the small hoops of reinforcing iron.

Spokes and Shaving

Your next job as an apprentice would be to split out the blanks for the spokes from straight-grained hickory, oak, or ash. Whereas the hub must be of wood that cannot be split, splitting out the spoke blanks actually ensures their strength. The grain of split stock will be continuous from end to end. To saw out the stock is to risk having pieces with a diagonal grain, a potentially disastrous weakness in a spoke.

Shaping spokes from seasoned stock calls for an experienced journeyman with a sharp drawknife. Holding the spoke in the long spoke vise, this journeyman trims away any wood that does not add to its strength. This reduces weight and increases the flexibility of the wheel near the rim. On the end of the spoke that will go into the hub, the wheelwright saws a tenon. The other, outer end is left unfinished to take the blows of the maul, for now each spoke must be driven securely into its mortice in the hub. When all have been forced home, the final length of each spoke can be gauged outward from the hub and the outer tenon marked and cut accordingly.

Fellies and Tires

The rims of the wheels are made up of sections called "fellies." They again must be of extremely tough wood—beech, ash, hickory, or oak—sawn out with the grain following its entire length. Each fellie must be morticed to take two spokes, so a twelve-spoke wheel will have six fellies. After the fellies are driven hard onto the spokes, there may still be visible gaps between the parts of the wheel—but not for long. Everything will be drawn together by the contraction of a hot tire of iron.

The tire can be made by a blacksmith, but the precise judgment of its circumference is best made by the wheelwright, for only the person who

The tire, expanded with heat from the fire, will shrink as it cools to bind the wheel together in an iron grip.

made the wheel knows how much compression the wood and the joints can take. After heating the tire in an open fire until it is hot enough to ignite a hickory splint, the wheelwright drops it over the wheel, immediately douses it with water, and then bangs it with a hammer to even out the remorseless contraction of the cooling iron ring. As the iron cools and the joints draw tight, the wheel becomes whole, ringing with tension, ready for the road, as strong as it can be, oak hard and ironbound.

THE MILLWRIGHT

Stop sometime where an old road crosses a river. Look upstream and, with luck, you will spot the tumbled remains of an old water-powered mill. Here, there once stood the oak equivalent of a forty-ton watch, a wooden machine that captured energy from the river and directed it to spin a grindstone or pull a saw blade. Little remains today to testify to the skill of the most sophisticated practical men of early America, the millwrights.

Few woodcrafters face challenges on such a massive scale as the millwright. Simply moving the huge timbers (a single one of which can outweigh two Buick Electras) calls for extraordinary ingenuity. Just finding trees big and straight enough can take months. Yet, although the timbers that make up the huge mill gears are correspondingly large, the joints between them must be perfect, with an allowable play of precisely zero.

Wheel Like a Heart

The heart of a mill is its waterwheel, and the heart of the wheel is its axle. This must be strong enough to support the four-ton dead load of the wheel and the weight and force of the rushing water as well. Only heart of white

The millwright repairing gears in Pyne's 1808 Microcosm.

A spider joint can be assembled within elongated mortices cut through the axle of the water wheel. When the last arm is driven through, the mortices will be wedged to lock it all together.

oak will do, 2 feet in diameter, 18 feet long. That's one mighty big piece of wood. You could plant a garden and see it come up in the time it takes to hew such a timber, and you could start a family and see your children half grown before it would be fully seasoned.

The axle of the waterwheel also serves as its hub and is home to a woodworking joint unique to the millwright's trade. Long ago millwrights developed a way to make an extraordinarily strong eight-spoked wheel by using only four long timbers that interlock inside the axle itself. They lap-jointed the timbers together where they crossed at their midpoint, making a joint that could then be reassembled within elongated mortices cut entirely through the axle. This unique joint allows all the spokes to radiate in the same plane and ensures that they can never slip or pull loose.

The lap joint can be cut with ordinary carpenters' tools, but morticing through 2 feet of white oak is another story. The millwright uses special heavy morticing chisels. A typical 1½-inch-wide millwright's chisel measures 19 inches long and weighs 3½ pounds—as much as a regular felling axe. It takes a powerful swing of a heavy mallet to drive one of these babies through the oak.

Inside the spider joint with the last two pieces cut and ready to go in.

Gearing Up

In all but the simplest mills, the millwright must now make the gears that will direct and temper the power captured by the waterwheel. It is a job that calls for super precision, for whereas the waterwheel must mesh only with the accommodating river, the gears will pit wood against wood in an endless search for flaws in craftsmanship or materials.

Every gear begins as a toothless wheel, for only when the gear is on its axle can the millwright situate the mortices for the replaceable applewood cog teeth. Turning the gear as if it were on a lathe, the millwright inscribes the center line for the cog mortices and then paces off their locations around its circumference with a pair of dividers. Boring and chopping the hundred mortices can take days, but the work can't be rushed. The hundred tapering shanks of the cogs (the tooth ends are still rough blocks at this point) must fit perfectly in their mortices. Should one of them come loose, the shock created by the sudden jump of the joining gear could break out the rest of the teeth before the frantic miller could close the sluice and stop the wheel.

An undershot water wheel in Franconia, Germany, that combines wheelwrighting with a lot of cooperage. The paddles are attached to the wheel with doubled-over split-oak saplings.

Only when all the cogs have been sledgehammered in around the wheel can they be shaped into proper gear teeth. Using a scribing tool driven into a stationary mill timber, the millwright marks the final circumference on the oversized cog blocks as the assistant slowly turns the wheel. When all have been sawn off on this line to their finished length, the millwright must then pace off the precise tooth spacing around the cogs, setting and resetting the dividers until the circle ends at the exact point where it began. Sometimes the needed adjustment is so small that it can only be made by filing away part of one of the divider points.

When the intervals are finally even, the millwright carefully pares away the tough wood to shape the teeth. All must be identical in shape and spacing, for if one stands out it will wear unevenly and the problem will get worse, not better, with time. When a tooth is out of step, it can be heard clearly when the mill is running and will "recite the craftsman's faults with every turn." The even rumble that is music to the miller's ear is achieved only through the unremitting diligence and care of the millwright.

THE COOPER'S TALE

The lyf so short, the craft so long to lerne.
– *Geoffrey Chaucer,* The Parliament of Fowls, *1380*

"Go watch George," they would say. "He's a real one!" I had scarcely been at work in Williamsburg for a day, and already three people had told me that I should go watch George Pettengell, the master cooper, at work. My awkwardness must have prompted them. So I went to see George. I stood in his shop and observed, looking for the secret of his ease and dexterity.

Master cooper George Pettengell "listing" a stave at Colonial Williamsburg. Behind him, his brother Jim hollows a stave at the shaving horse as Lew LeCompte tightens the hoops on a large cask.

In the few light hours of a winter's day, George Pettengell can transform a stack of rough split-oak boards into a liquid-tight container worthy of 54 gallons of the finest brew. His tools, which have served two generations of coopers before him, are highly specialized implements, strange even to the experienced woodworker. Perhaps the tools are the answer. If only I had such fine tools, then perhaps I could do as well.

I watched George at work. The blade of his axe is long and thin. With it he chops along the grain to "list" the split-oak board to the double-tapered, bevel-edged shape of a stave. His aim is uncannily accurate, yet he works with the speed of a hungry man at supper. Could it be the length or the sharpness of his blade that makes the cut so smooth? Perhaps the wood is the answer. Even the few pieces that he tosses into the firewood box seem flawless to me.

Stave after stave takes shape, each following the unseen pattern. Nothing guides the guillotine edge of the axe except his arm, nothing defines the shape of the stave except his eye. Now he takes the bundle of listed staves to his "draw bench" or "shaving horse." This foot-operated vise holds the stave at just the proper height and inclination for him to shape the outer and inner faces with a drawknife. On the convex face of the stave he uses a large, straight knife and with a few long strokes shapes the outside to a curve that gradually tightens at each end of the stave where the diameter of the barrel is smallest.

For the inside of the stave, he uses a U-shaped hollowing knife. Its curve is roughly equivalent to the radius needed for the interior of the stave. Only a curved knife could form the hollow, but, just as with the other tools, nothing measures or controls the depth or length of the cut except his eyes and hands.

After he has listed, rounded, and hollowed them with freehand axes and knives, now he takes the staves to a huge, upside-down plane. This behemoth, standing with one end on the floor and the other on two legs, is the cooper's jointer. Sliding the staves down its slope, sending paper-thin curls to the floor of the shop, he trues each mating surface. Anyone could make one perfectly straight edge with this giant. But where is the guide? Where is the fence to hold each stave at the proper angle to make it match its neighbor in a watertight seal? These are the critical surfaces—any error here and the container simply won't hold water. Search in vain for such external guides, for they exist only in the skill of the craftsman.

Raising

Compared with shaping the staves, the process of assembling or "raising" them into a barrel is as mechanical as arithmetic. It takes know-how and strength, but basically it's simple addition. Holding a hoop, George deftly fills it in with staves until the circle is closed. One end of the barrel is

now together, each stave forced against the next like an arch composed entirely of keystones. In order to draw the far end of the cask together, forming the bulging barrel shape, he first softens the staves by building a small fire of shavings within the splay-bottomed cylinder. When the oak is heated through, George and his younger brother Jim drive on a series of successively smaller wooden "trussing" hoops until the barrel takes shape.

George and Jim drive down the trussing hoop to bring the staves together.

Now George reaches for his most unusual and highly specialized tools of all: the ones used to prepare the ends of the cask to take the heads. The tightly curved, short-handled cooper's adz, the sideways curved "topping" or "sun" plane, the "howell" and "croze" with their half-moon fences that reach inside to level and cut the grooves for the head—each takes its turn until the barrel is done.

The Sum of Experience

I don't even have to try these tools to guess the truth. The secret of George Pettengell's speed and grace is really no secret at all. Axe or piano, block plane or jet plane, the tools are only as good as the person who uses them. I have been watching the results of over thirty years of professional experience. When someone makes skilled work "look easy," the secret is something much more costly than the finest tools—it's time.

Browsing through the stacks at the mill.

ROBINSON'S MILL

No road signs will lead you to the Robinson brothers' sawmill. Someone must tell you which turns to take until you finally spot the stacks of lumber climbing above the undergrowth. If the cable is not locked across the rutted dirt road, you may enter into a maze of lumber stacks. Some piles sit low, dark, and gray; others stand bright and tall. Stacks of poplar boards are cream-colored with mocha puddles of heartwood. Oak is pungent and looks inflamed; beech boards are always convoluted. The highest stacks are of pine planks, raw and pink, towering against the blue sky.

Along the edge of the woods stand rusting giants of turn-of-the-century woodworking. A huge vertical band mill leans toward a post oak like an Easter Island statue. Its huge wheels are at least 5 feet in diameter. On its side is a brass plate bearing the patent dates: 1894, 1898, 1900, 1906. The band mill is flanked by the rusting and broken resaws that once sliced the wide planks into the narrower widths of building timber. A few charred posts from the old sheds still stand about.

In the distance you hear the high hum of the saw fall into a moaning tear as another log takes a ride into the spinning teeth. This is the best time, when you can hear the brothers working down at the mill, leaving you free to explore among the timber stacks without help. What have they been cutting? No rosewood from Pernambuco or teak from Sarawak, but perhaps an exotic yard tree, a prime white oak, a cypress, or a walnut has found its way to this yard and now lies cut and drying here under the sky.

As you wander between the stacks, a web of blackberry vines crunches underfoot. (Exploring here is always well rewarded in July.) Walking down the rutted road around water-filled potholes, you pass sheds made from boards nailed to quartets of hickory trees. Poison ivy–covered, blackened dregs of lumber stacks that even the kindling scavengers pass over lurk between the trees. The snow begins.

The closer you get to the mill, the more you notice the light dust of sawdust-snow falling from the sky. The source of the dust, the mill, hunkers in the center of the clearing, a sprawling, tin-roofed shed overtopped by a Matterhorn of bright yellow sawdust. In the winter these mountains steam from the composting deep within. They say these sawdust mountains become hollow as they rot, and that climbers can fall in and be swallowed up. Those who dare to scale the 40 feet to the summit are on a level with the tops of a pair of bull pines where the local turkey vultures roost.

The shed is a remarkable organism, looking as though ultraviolet light and lightning bolts initiated a primitive life-form out of a jumble of sticks—and then gave up. The sawyer, the eldest of the elderly brothers, works in the heart of the jumble, eyeing each log and choosing the slices with tugs of the hydraulic handles. One of his brothers feeds him logs with a smoking, roaring forklift still painted gray from the days it spent pushing wrecked Navy dive bombers into the waters of the wartime Pacific.

As the boards fall free of the blade, a small, old man—not one of the three brothers—stacks them into piles separated by crosswise stickers. He is missing half of his left forearm, the stump covered by a leather cup. He never speaks. You hear it was a hunting accident that took his arm away, and not the mill, but the sight gives you a chilling respect for the flying chains, gears, belts, and blades.

The noise of the saw masks all sounds short of shouting. The little dog comes up behind you without warning and sticks his nose into the back of your leg. You jump, startled, and he bounds away, hopeful eye still upon you. He follows you at a distance until you coax him close enough to pet.

The brothers go on about their work until you can catch the eye of one or the other. Timing is everything. They may not wish to be stopped just now. Perhaps they aren't exactly sure who you are. Have they dealt with you before? Rough and old though they look, they are shy. Once you know them well enough, though, conversation becomes easy. You walk back up the road to load your timber, wishing you could talk with them today. How did that guy really lose his arm?

Returning with the boards, you wait until the youngest brother comes over to measure the planks and calculate your bill. He measures out the widths with his Doyle timber rule, figures a bit on his paper, and hands you the total. He takes your money and makes any change out of an old ammo box kept in the forklift. "What are you building?" he always asks. He will tell the others later, over dinner, what their wood is going to become, completing the circle.

The Gunsmith

Stolen from the subscriber on his march from Augusta to Williamsburg . . . a very neat rifle gun. The stock of sugar-tree, curled—made pretty dark by aqua fortis.
– John Grattan, advertisement in the Virginia Gazette, *April 12, 1776*

I do not know if Mr. Grattan ever caught up with the man that stole his rifle, but I can well imagine the results of such a meeting. This was no government-issue musket, but a handcrafted flintlock longrifle—an American original, a work of supreme craftsmanship and artistry—and Lord help the man caught trying to steal it.

No ordinary gun, the rifle was made by no ordinary craftsman. The gunsmith combines the skills of blacksmith, machinist, locksmith, engraver, sculptor, and woodcarver, bringing wood, iron, and brass together in a creation of precision and beauty.

Gunsmith George Suiter in his shop at Colonial Williamsburg.

"Sugar Tree, Curled"

Although it may take several weeks to forge and machine the barrel and flintlock mechanisms for a new rifle, the gunsmith's work on the stock will have begun years earlier. The fit (and function) of the iron and brass parts of the rifle will be ruined if the wooden stock is not perfectly seasoned, so the gunsmith must set aside the wood for three to seven years before using it. Although some might stock a rifle with cherry, walnut, or plain maple, the American classic is that tough stuff from the sugartree, curly maple.

Beginning with the pile of roughly shaped blanks, the gunsmith must plan to use the wood to its best advantage. The gunsmith looks for decorative "figure" in the wood—convolutions of the grain that will be displayed in the broad butt of the rifle. In the "wrist," however, where the breech of the barrel, the firing mechanism, and the grip of the right hand converge, there can be no flaw that might weaken the wood at this crucial point.

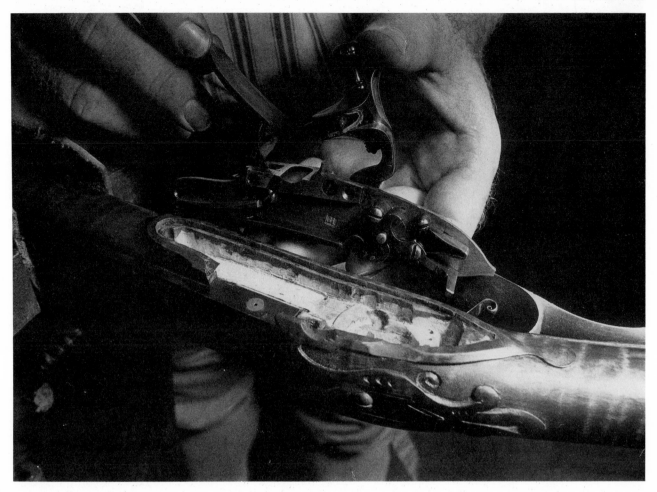

Lock, Stock, and Barrel

The gunsmith's first task in assembling the rifle is to bed the tapered, octagonal barrel into the roughly shaped stock. After it has been roughed in with gouges and chisels, the final approach to a perfect fit is made by trial and error. Coating the barrel with soot from a candle, the gunsmith tries it into place and then removes wood only where the transferred soot marks indicate interference. Painstaking but positive, this same method can be used to fit all of the remaining metal parts. It's worth it. Unlike a tea service or writing desk, a rifle made with lesser workmanship can be fatal.

Using the barrel as the baseline, the gunsmith must now fit the lock and trigger mechanisms, not just into the wood but also into a precise working relationship to one another. Scratching the outline of the lockplate onto the wood, the gunsmith begins the hollowing—and faces yet another challenge. Hollowing the stock to house these workings weakens it at precisely the point where strength is most needed. Leaving every bit of wood possible, the gunsmith fits the lock into the stock like a hand into a glove.

Inletting the lock into the stock requires the gunsmith to remove no more wood than absolutely necessary to maintain the strength of the firearm.

Next, the gunsmith inlets the trigger and the many brass mountings with equal precision. These brass plates, unlike the finished iron of the lock, can be filed flush with the wood around them, melding the two surfaces so that they appear as one. Each of the wood screws used to fasten these brass plates must go back into the same hole from which it was removed—because even the screws are custom made, the threads hand filed.

Bas Relief

The decorative work on a rifle serves not just to ornament the surface but to unify the whole. Instead of incising patterns into the wood, the gunsmith creates the interlacing C and S scrolls by the much more difficult method of cutting away the background and leaving the patterns as raised figures. After lining out the boundaries with gouges, the smith pares away the background to a constant depth. Even in the carving, the potentially bulky "wrist" remains the focus of attention. As master gunsmith Wallace Gusler pointed out, "You have to try to carry your lines through this area. The carving makes it look slender, and gives the gun grace."

Even the finishing of a curly maple stock is something special. The aqua fortis that made the stolen rifle "pretty dark" is nitric acid, which, when mixed with iron filings, makes a remarkable stain. When the gunsmith paints the stock with this mixture, it seems to do no more than wet the pale blond wood. But when the surface is heated by holding a red-hot iron bar over it, the wood blossoms into a deep reddish brown. Rubbing with linseed oil brings depth and finish to the wood and life to one of our forefathers' most treasured possessions.

MAYHEW AND THE DARK SIDE OF WOODCRAFT

In 1859, novelist George Eliot penned the classic romantic word-picture of the village joiner's shop, a place where: "The afternoon sun was warm on the five workmen there, busy upon doors and window-frames and wainscoting. . . . The slanting sunbeams shone through the transparent shavings that flew before the steady plane, and lit up the fine grain of the oak panelling which stood propped against the wall."

Eliot goes on to add dogs dozing on piles of shavings amid the honest, hearty workmen who sing aloud in the sunbeams. Surely life was better in those days before trade unions sapped the vitality of the noble workman. But contrast Eliot's bucolic images in *Adam Bede* with the descriptions of real London woodworking shops of the 1850s, as recorded by social reformer Henry Mayhew:

The shop in which I work is for all the world like a prison—the silent system is as strictly carried out there as in a model gaol. If a man was to ask any common question of his neighbor, . . . he would be discharged there and then. If a journeyman makes the least mistake, he is packed off just the same.

No sunshine and singing here. Country carpenters from all over England traditionally went to London for a few years to refine their skills as "improvers." They then returned to their towns, taking with them the London styles and standards. But by the mid-nineteenth century, something had gone wrong, and these countrymen increasingly were pulled into a web of murderous sweatshops that starved the workmen and cheated the customers.

Quality was not of the least concern to the speculative developers who saw a gold mine in the growing demand for suburban London housing. Honest craftsmen were powerless against the laissez-faire culture of greed. "The public is being fleeced . . . to an extent that builders alone can know. . . . The houses are not safe to live in." Said one master builder, "Honesty is now almost impossible among us."

Skill and experience gained with age were no longer valued. The new masters wanted only the speed and strength of youth, and men were forced to conceal any indication of advancing age. "I used to wear glasses in one employ, and others did the same, and the foreman was a good man to the men as well as to the master; and if the master was coming, he used to sing out 'Take those sashes out of the way,' and so we had time to whip off our glasses, and the master didn't know we were forced to use them; but when he did find out, by coming into the shop unawares, he discharged two men."

Some of the loss of value and dignity in these men's work and lives was accounted to the introduction of steam-powered machinery. One of the house joiners interviewed by Mayhew recalled how mechanical planers gradually appropriated their work. At first the men welcomed the machines because they were used for only the lowliest tasks, such as tonguing and grooving floorboards. "The joiners thought nothing at first of the planing of these boards by machinery, as only a certain class were put upon sash planing—it was beneath their dignity, and I have known men leave a shop rather than do it." As the machines became more sophisticated, though, they took over more complex and highly valued work like the planing of ornamental mouldings, and they began to displace even the most skilled men.

The cabinetmaking trade did not escape the sweatshop shoddiness either. While some cabinetmakers remained "honorable," serving customers with a reasonable eye for quality, many labored in the "slaughterhouses" making cheap furniture for gullible people. "The deal's nailed

A country carpenter coming to grief in London in 1861 might have to sell his tools to the vendors in Petticoat Lane. The misfortune of one might bring opportunity for another; the used tools could be bought as cheaply as they were sold.

"Advice to 'those about to Marry'—Buy Cheap Furniture"—from George Cruikshank, The Comic Almanack, *1852.*

together, and the veneer's dabbed on, and if the deal's covered, why the thing passes. The worst of it is that people don't understand either good work or good wood." Women and children were exploited as well. A number of women told Mayhew how they would stand at the bench with their young children, polishing furniture from four in the morning until seven in the evening with no food, drink, or rest. Even with their husbands fully employed, they could not earn enough to live on. This intolerable exploitation could not be sustained, and it pushed thousands into the labor movements of the second half of the nineteenth century.

But by the end of the century, the anguish of those years had been quickly forgotten by those who did not endure it. The truculence and swagger of the newly empowered union men encouraged romantic nostalgia and sermons such as we find in turn-of-the-century cabinetmaking manuals: "The only true way to success is that the heart be in the work; toiling not just merely for the 'standard wage,' nor creating a piece of work only to 'sell,' but to last." This is true enough, but it is easier to say when your stomach is full and your children have a chance to outlive you.

4

Furniture

Katherina: I knew you at the first, you were a moveable.

Petruchio: Why, what's a moveable?

Katherina: A joint stool.

Petruchio: Thou has hit it: come sit on me!

– William Shakespeare, *The Taming of the Shrew*, 1593

[overleaf]
The Danish folding chair, shown both open and partially closed in this double exposure.

FOLDING FOLK CHAIRS

This interesting chair is called a faldstool or Danish curule. The fingers of its curved sides scissor open to form either a seat or the base for a table. I enjoy making these curved pieces with an adz. Basically, you chop the curve into the broad faces of a wide, thick plank and then separate it into individual pieces with straight saw cuts. Alternatively, you may find it easier to use a thin-bladed saw to cut the curves as a series of nesting pieces.

You will need to start with a good, hard 2 by 12 (or a pair of 2 by 6s) to make the sides. Lay out the bends on both edges of the plank with a long rule. Then draw square lines across the faces at 4-inch intervals. These lines will guide the saw cuts that will in turn act as depth gauges to guide and ease your axe work. A firewood-cutting bucksaw is a good tool for this part of the job. At the same time that you cut these depth gauges, mark and saw the shoulders for the tenons on the ends of these pieces. Lean the plank up against a timber to get a good working angle and adz away chunks of wood, always adzing from the shallower saw cut to the deeper one. You can do the same job with a small hatchet.

Finish up the surface with some cross-grain planing. When you are satisfied that you need cut no more, draw square lines across the faces to

You can quickly make the curved side pieces of the chair by shaping a broad plank and then sawing it into narrow slices. An adz works well for this job.

Saw the shoulders for the tenons across the ends of the plank before sawing it into individual pieces.

guide the placement of the pivot holes. Then draw guide lines for the rips down the length of the plank and start sawing. Keep the newly divided pieces together as a pair if their grain has a distinctive character that will make them appear as a unit in the assembled chair.

Once the pieces are apart, bore the pivot holes and finish all the tenons on the ends. The header brackets need a row of mortices down their length to match the tenons. Space these mortices to account for the thickness of any washers you might use between the fingers.

The stretchers forming the seat are identical, but, like the sides, they face in alternate directions. Make them uniform by shaping a single plank and then sawing it up into individual pieces. The angle to which you want the legs to scissor open will determine the angle that you need to cut on the end of the board. Set the side assemblies together with their pivot rod in place and spread them to the opening you desire. Span the opening between the two seat holes and record the angle of the intersection with a bevel gauge. Without moving anything, measure both the distance between these two holes and the distance between one hole and the surface of the wood on the opposite piece.

These measurements will now enable you to lay out the seat slat plank to fit the desired leg spread. Scribe a line across one end of the plank to mark the position of the holes for the end pivot. Now measure out half of the distance between the two seat holes to locate the center hole. Finally, measure out the distance from a seat hole to the opposite wood surface to locate the *center* of the bevel on the end. Saw the bevel, saw the pieces apart, drill the holes, and put it all together.

I think this would make a good base for a table as well. This particular piece could be made as one or the other, but there is another European design that can become one or the other as you wish.

Mortice a header to join with the tenons on the side pieces.

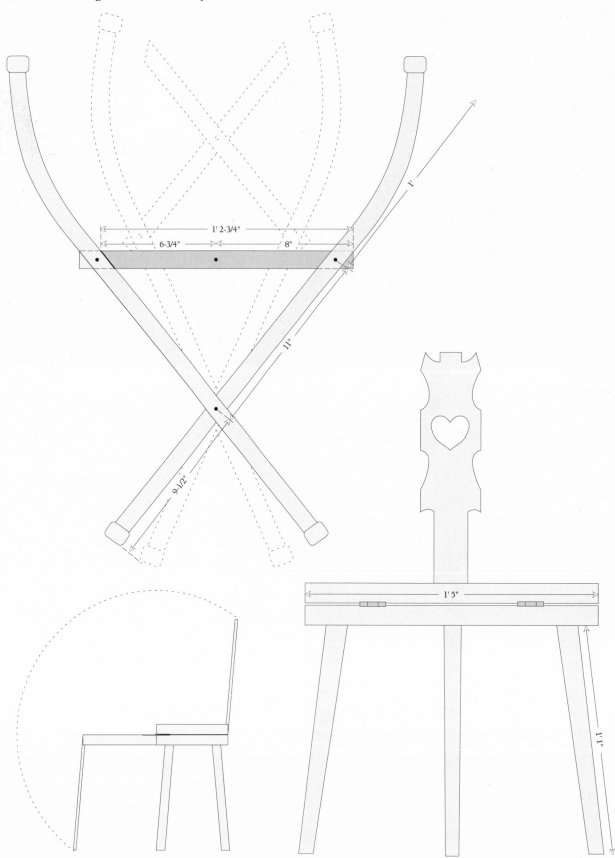

The folding chair and the table/chair.

CHAIR/TABLE

As with anything that converts from one thing to another, this chair/table combines about equal measures of utility and cuteness. It is a Danish folk design and has a definite appeal for anyone living in a small space. It's easy and quick to make. The only hang-up might be finding or making hinges attractive enough to be exposed when the piece is in its table mode. I would like to see a design that uses wooden hinges.

For the moment, though, here's how to proceed with iron hinges. When the chair is a table, it is 17 inches in diameter and 1½ inches thick. This means you need a length of oak plank 8½ inches wide. This is a good width because it is narrow enough that you can split it from a log rather than having to saw it or buy it. The legs and back are also of oak (or ash, or something else hard and strong).

The table/chair in both positions in this double exposure. Kids love this one, but the back is fragile.

Saw or chop two semicircles from the plank. Of the four faces of these two semicircles, only one will face the floor at all times. Choose the worst of the four faces for this duty. It is easier to set in the hinges now than it will be later on, so butt the two semicircles together, good faces up, separated by a four-fold sheet of paper, and set the hinges in place. Place the hinges so that they will not intersect the legs. Trace around the hinges to mark where you will chisel their seats to make them flush with the surface. The paper spacers will help to ensure that the chair continues to unfold into a flat table even if the wood should swell with humidity. (The wood will get fatter but the iron hinge will not.)

Chisel the insets for the hinges by first striking their outlines and then hatching the surface to a constant depth with measured strikes of the mallet and chisel. Fit the hinges into place and drill pilot holes for the nails or screws. (You could use butt hinges, but they are a vastly more modern design than surface-mounted butterfly or dovetail hinges.) Fasten the hinges into place and flip the circle over to put on the legs.

Check again to see which of the two underside semicircles has the poorer face. This is the surface that should receive the legs. The legs are of the same hardwood used for the plank, gently tapering from top to bottom. They must splay out to the sides, so either set a bevel gauge or saw an angle guide from scrap wood to steer the auger as you bore the holes. Bore from the bottom up through the top, setting a waste piece beneath it to prevent splintering.

The legs are square, but their tenons are round, so saw the shoulders and split away the wood until you can make the final fitting with a rasp. Set the tenons into their mortices and drive the legs home only far enough to ensure that they are properly aligned. On each you will see that the shoulder of the tenon is at an angle to the surface of the plank. Scribe the shoulder to a perfect parallel by using a pair of dividers or a wooden spacer that rides on the plank and marks up onto the shoulder. Pull the leg back out and resaw the shoulder to this new line, then chisel and rasp the remaining wood.

Before you drive the leg in for the final time, saw a slot in the end of the tenon to take the wedge. Be sure to align the slot in each leg so that the wedge will go in *across* the grain of the plank. Drive the leg to a flush fit. When all the legs are so fitted, you can measure an equal distance up from the plank on all three legs to mark the ends for sawing. Measuring this way ensures that the seat will sit level. Flip the thing over and drive the wedges into the protruding ends of the legs. Saw them off flush with the place where you sit.

The back of the chair (which doubles as a leg) is pretty weak in this design, so select a piece of wood with a continuous grain and fasten it securely to the plank with large screws or blind-wedged pegs and glue. Cut its length to correspond with that of the legs and have a seat.

THE CHAIRMAKERS

When great ships crossed the oceans by the force of the winds, two brothers sailed to the New World to seek their fortunes. Both chose to follow the trade of the chairmaker. Both believed in the value of hard work and diligence. But one remained in the city where they landed and the other continued west into the mountains.

The brother in the mountains soon found a teacher: an old country chairmaker in need of a helper. The old man taught him how to seek the straight-grained hickory in the forest and how to fell it and carry it down the mountainside on his shoulder without getting killed. Back at the work-yard, he showed his assistant how to split the wood into billets, how to shape it with a hand axe, and how to shave the fresh, cream-colored wood into rounds ready for the bending frames.

The city brother, having found a master of his own, soon signed his papers of apprenticeship. His education began down at the docks, where he learned how to haggle over the price of mahogany logs with the timber merchants. He learned to negotiate with the carters to haul the timbers up the cobblestone streets to the saw yard. He learned to make a place for himself in the competitive hustle of a busy city shop.

Different Strokes

Far from those noisy streets, the country brother's next job was to help his aged mentor bend the chairbacks. Together they forced the still green wood into work-worn bending frames. They left them there for weeks to dry into a permanent set, the grain of the hickory following the curves of the frame with undiminished strength.

City brother was helping shape the backs of chairs as well. He pulled his end of a narrow-bladed frame saw to track the curves struck by the master's graphite pencil. Stealing quick glances away from the relentless advance of the blade, he watched the master lay out the cutting patterns on the costly planks so that they meshed together like spoons in a drawer.

Although both masters left the actual sawing and chisel work to the younger men, they personally marked out all of the joints for each of their chairs. One wielded a gauge made of iron nails set into a hickory staff, the other used one of rosewood, brass, and steel; but they were identical in their precision. The country master's gauge was permanently set, because the design of his chairs remained the same year after year. The city master's gauge, however, was easily adjustable with the turn of a screw—ready to move with the currents of fashion.

City chair.

Country chair.

[opposite]

Lay out the mortices and tenons on all the pieces before turning them to shape on the lathe. You can see that I got a little ahead of myself on this one.

Tavern table in the works. (Any horizontal surface becomes filled, even before it's finished.)

Function at the Junction

The mortice-and-tenon joints cut by the city chairmaker and his country brother were the same in theory but different in execution. The city brother chopped exact rectangular pockets and sawed precisely matching mahogany tongues—simple shapes driven together and locked with pegs and glue. The country brother's mortices were but single auger holes bored into the uprights, and his tenons on the stretcher ends were cut with a common pocket knife. Superficially simple, these country joints were actually more complex than the glued joints of any city chair. Rather than shaping plain cylindrical tenons, the country chairmaker quickly but carefully whittled the ends of each stretcher to an oval swelling. These dry, bulbous ends, when driven into the less seasoned uprights, would soon be locked forever in place by the death grip of the shrinking wood surrounding them.

Although his chair was not yet complete, the city brother was now done with his part of the work. He was learning only the trade of the chair framer. The strong mahogany frame now went to the carver and *his* apprentices, who would in turn send it to the finishers, who would then pass it along to the upholsterer for the addition of a leather seat.

But country brother was back in the woods. He felled a small hickory tree and pulled its bark off in long, heavy strips that he coiled around his hand. Back at the cabin, he shaved the bark thinner and to a consistent width. "Over two, under two," he counted to himself as he wove the herringbone-patterned chair seat. The seat was still rough-looking when he finished it. The ultimate polish would be applied by its new owner during the first year of sitting on it.

Two chairs with different destinies—one bound for the porch of a farmer's house, the other for the parlor of a merchant's mansion. No one could mistake one chair for the other. But both were precisely suited to the materials and skills available and to the wants and means of their prospective owners.

Two brothers, far apart, yet united in the universal community of craftsmanship.

TAVERN TABLE

A tavern table is little and low, with a low stretcher to get your feet off of the drafty floor. This little tavern table is a good start for the novice furniture maker. It's a simple job with a little mortice-and-tenon work, a little turning. As in all such work, we will cut the joints first, before turning the legs, to prevent the rough handling necessary for morticing from tearing up the turnings. And, as with all mortice-and-tenon work, the morticing gauge is the key.

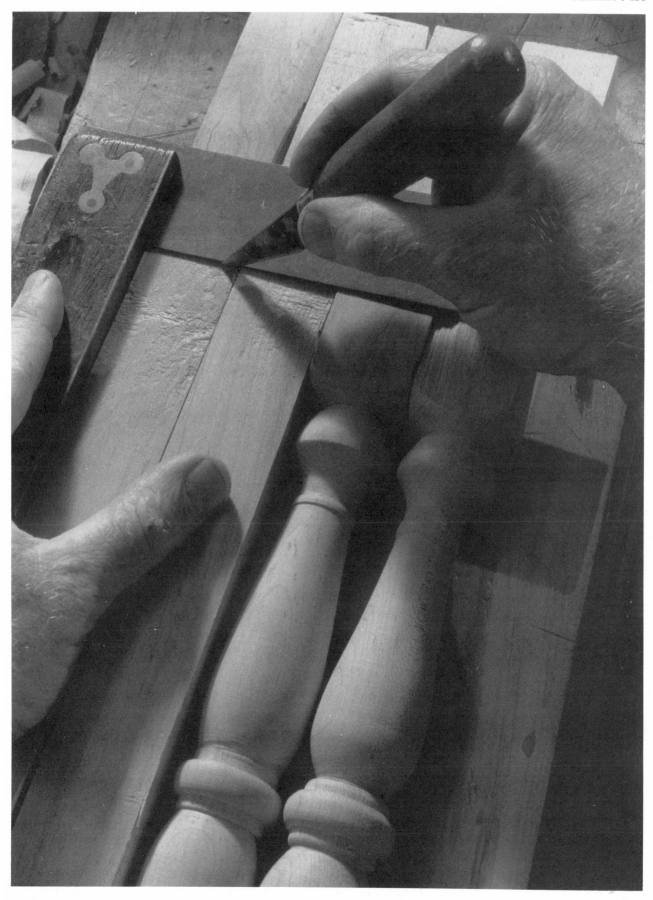

Legs

Make the legs of pine, planing them into 1¾-inch square billets. The square sections will look better if the rings of the wood are diagonal to the facets. This will give some nice edge grain to all surfaces. Lay out the length of all the mortices at once by squaring across all four legs as you hold them together on the bench. Set the two points of the morticing gauge to the width of the morticing chisel (⅜ inch) and to the offset from the outside faces of the legs. I have set the rails flush with the faces of the legs, but you may find it more attractive to inset them ⅛ inch or more.

For the heavier mortices in the timbers of the lathe and the loom, it was easiest to remove a lot of the wood with the auger. For small mortices like this, it is faster to do all the work with the morticing chisel. Start the chisel a little bit in from the ends of the mortice and drive it in. Move it along a little and drive it in again, repeating until you are close to the other end. Work your way back down again and pry out the chips. Because these two mortices converge within the leg, you should cut the first one only to where it begins to intersect the second mortice (the one you have not cut yet). If you were to cut the first mortice to full depth, it would leave a hollow under the chiseling of the second mortice and cause splintering when you break through. Finally, trim the ends of both mortices with a single vertical cut levered into the center.

Rails

Although the lower rails are plain rectangles, the upper rails receive a moulding along the lower corner. Whether you use a moulding plane or a scratch stock, you may want to go ahead and mold the whole length before you cut the stock into four pieces. Start using the moulding plane at the far end of the piece and slowly work your way back as the moulding takes shape. When you have molded the stock and cut it to the right lengths, hold the appropriate pairs together and lay out the tenon shoulders as one. (Layout and joint-cutting is easier and more accurate on unmolded, rectangular stock. You should judge each job as to whether molding first will save you any work over molding the individual pieces after the joints are cut.) Adjust the offset of the morticing gauge if necessary and scratch the thickness of the tenons around the ends of all the pieces, being sure always to gauge from the face side. Saw the shoulders and cheeks of the tenons, then miter the ends with a chisel so that both of the converging tenons can use the full depth of their respective mortices. This is that same equalization of strength that made the wonderful one-hoss shay last so long.

[opposite]

Lay out the width and location of the mortice with the double-toothed morticing gauge. Always gauge from the "face" side, usually the side that will be seen; obviously the splintered area on the left should not face outward on the finished table.

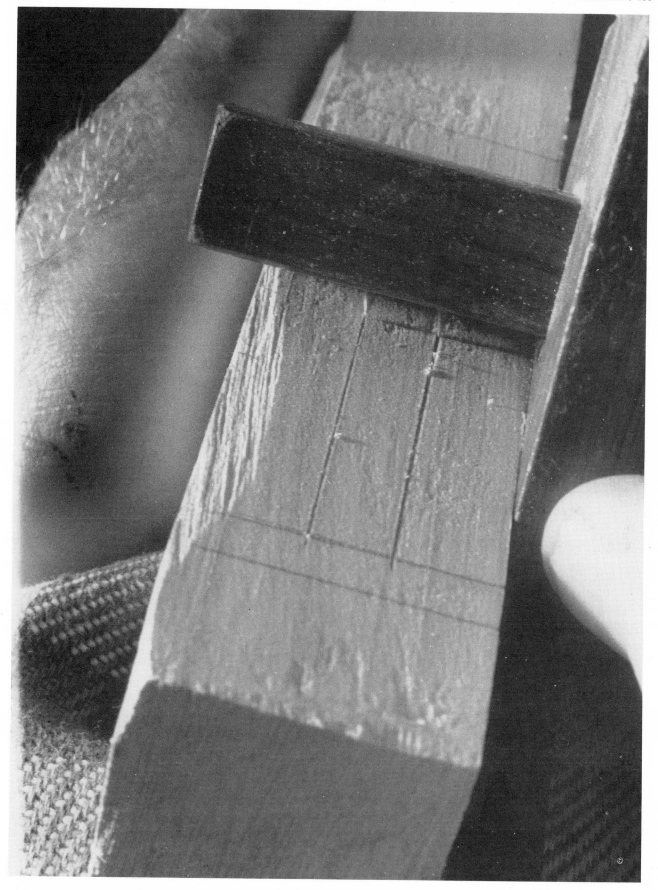

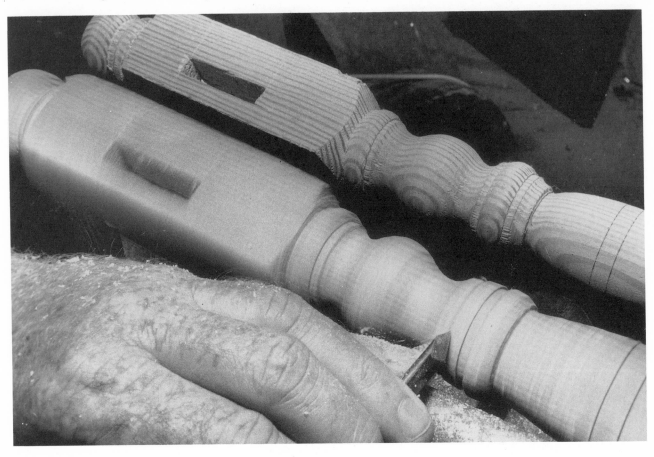

After morticing the blank leg, mount it in the lathe and turn it to the finished shape. After you have roughed the first one in, you can use it as a pattern to guide the rest.

Turning

Once all the mortice-and-tenon joints are fitted, you can go ahead and turn the legs on the lathe. One easy way to find the center of square stock (usually you draw diagonals connecting opposing corners) is to use a single-toothed gauge set to approximately half the thickness of the stock. Gauge in on the end grain from all sides and you will have the center well defined.

Once the work is spinning on the lathe, make your first cuts with a skew chisel at the intersections of the square and round sections. This first, deep cut will keep you from splintering off the corners of the square section as you turn the round sections. If you have not done enough wood turning to confidently shape the pieces by eye, make either a paper pattern or find an existing leg to copy. Dividers and calipers will bring precision to your work by locating and setting the diameter of salient points down the length of the work. Into the initial cylinder, you simply make a series of sizing cuts at each shoulder, high point, and low point of the pattern with a parting tool. Once these dimensions are set and the shape blocked in, you finish the shapes with the gouges and skew chisels. After turning, reassemble the joints, drawbore and peg them, and there you have the frame.

The Top

The tavern table top is usually small enough that it can be made from a single piece. All you need to do is mold the edges, again using either the scratch stock or moulding plane. Take care to mold the end grain of the top first. The end grain is always likely to break out at the end, but if the broken ends will later be taken away when you mold the long grain, it matters not. The best way to join a cheap tavern table top to the frame is by nailing down through the top. If this is too crude for your taste, try boring some angled holes up through the inside corners of the top rails that will enable you to fasten them to the top with unseen screws. Nails, crude nails, are the most common solution.

Miter off the end of the tenons so that they can both reach as deeply as possible in the converging mortices. The idea is to maximize the gluing surface.

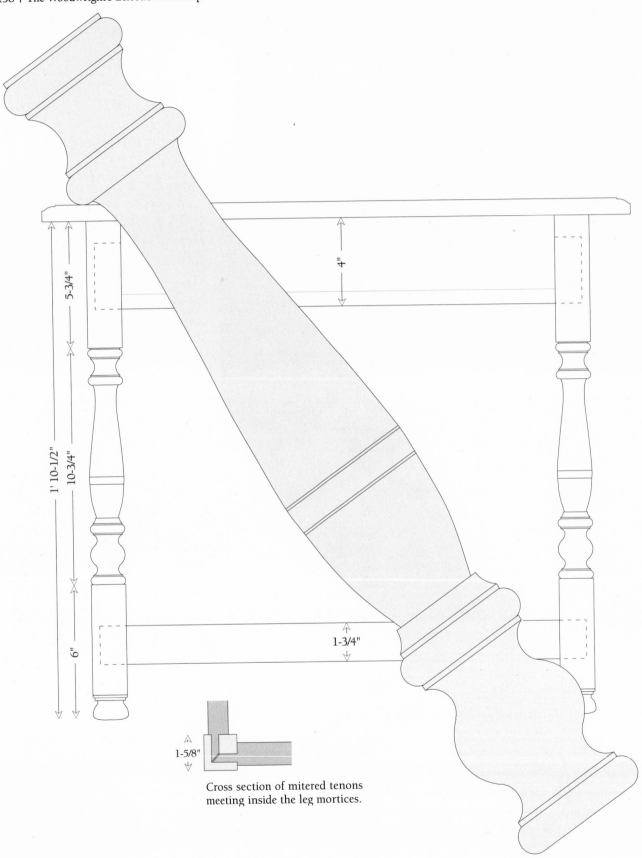

5-3/4"

4"

1' 10-1/2"

10-3/4"

6"

1-3/4"

1-5/8"

Cross section of mitered tenons
meeting inside the leg mortices.

The simple tavern table.

BUTTERFLY TABLE

This butterfly table is a classic. The splay of the legs gives stability to the broad top, which is supported by the outspread wings. These same wings can swing in and allow the leaves to fold down so that the table can fit in a corner. A little drawer under the top keeps cards or sotweed at the ready. Russell Kettell, the author of *Pine Furniture of Early New England*, found this design so attractive that he included a maple butterfly table in his book, on the grounds that one of the wings happened to be pine.

The Frame

You can make the frame of this table in the same way that you did the previous tavern table. The only difference is that you must cut angled shoulders on the tenons of some of the rails to create the outward splay. The mortices that mate with these angle-shouldered tenons also need to be cut at the reciprocal angle. Setting your bevel gauge so that the blade extends from both sides of the body of the gauge will give you both angles—one to guide the saw for the tenon, the other to guide the chisel for the mortice.

The butterfly tavern table, metamorphosed from the caterpillar of a log.

Rule Joint

Making the rule joints for the leaves of the table top is both easier and harder than it looks. The part that looks hard—getting the quarter-round shapes of the joint—is easy compared to the challenge of locating the hinges so that they will have the proper action. This rule joint is basically a quarter of a 1-inch-diameter circle with the axle of the hinge at the center. As with most any moulding, you can find old planes (called table planes) made specifically to cut the quarter-round and hollow portions of this joint. But these are also about the easiest mouldings of all to make with scratch stocks. Again, the trick is to rough in the profile with quicker cutting tools and use the scratch stocks just for shaping the last 1/16 inch or so.

For the concave part of the joint on the dropleaf, use the marking gauge to outline the area 1/2 inch back from the lower corner on both edges. (You should, as always, gauge down from the face, or top side, to lay out these measurements, but I will describe the dimensions from the bottom to eliminate any confusion resulting from table tops of varying thicknesses.) Draw a diagonal between these two lines and get rid of all the wood outside the diagonal with a drawknife or plane. Now, starting at the far end and working your way back (just as you do with the moulding plane), gouge a hollow down the length of the joint just shy of the finished measurement. Even when you use moulding planes rather than scratch stocks,

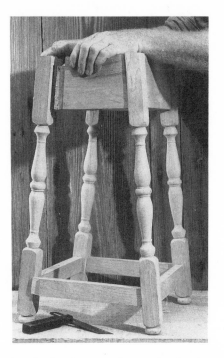

Use the bevel gauge to lay out the sloping shoulders of the tenons and mortice the legs at the reciprocal angle to allow the tenons to go straight in.

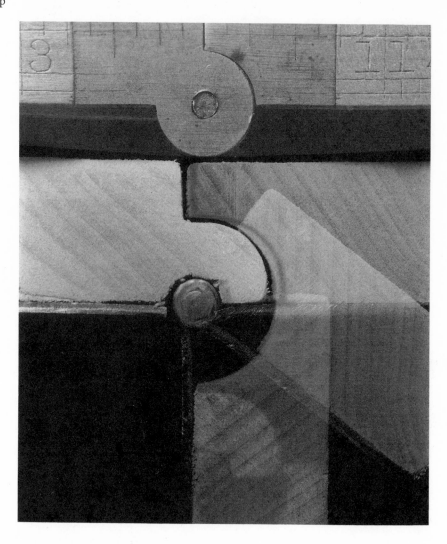

The rule joint gets its name from the old folding ruler. The inset hinge lets the concave portion of the leaf roll off the quarter-round support of the main top.

roughing in the work with faster-cutting freehand tools will make the job easier on you and the tools.

On the main part of the table, where the convex element resides, you again measure ½ inch up from the lower edge and ½ inch back onto the top surface. Then cut down with a rabbet plane to remove a rectangular section ½ inch back from the edge and ¼ inch deep. You can use the same rabbet plane to round it off roughly before finishing it with the scratch stock.

Hinges made for rule joints are different from common leaf hinges, and not only because one leaf is longer than the other. The screw holes are different as well, being countersunk on the opposite side from the raised hinge knuckle. You can buy these hinges from some of the mail-order houses listed in the appendix. Set the hinges across the joint on the underside of the table top, with the long leaf of the hinge on the dropleaf side of the joint. You must locate the axis of the hinge at the center of the circle formed by the convex and concave elements of the joint so that they will roll past one another, not open up. Some clearance is necessary for the

joint to move freely, so slip a folded piece of paper in between the pieces to space out the joint. Try a mock operation of the joint to make sure you understand how it works.

This scratch stock is made to finish the concave portion of the rule joint after it has been roughed in with gouges and perhaps a plane. You can see from the teeth that the blade is made from an old handsaw.

When you have the hinges properly situated, scribe around them with a scratch awl and prick four extra little marks at the corners of the barrel of each hinge. You must now countersink the hinge to a depth dependent upon the make of the hinge, the thickness of the wood, and the geometry of the joint. You may have to mortice only for the barrel to get the proper action. If you need to countersink the leaves of the hinge as well, simply saw down a bit on either edge of the needed recess and pare out the depth with a chisel. Put the hinges into place again and test the operation before you put screws into the wood.

The Ellipse

The elliptical shape of this table is best laid out and cut after you have completed the rule joints. Everyone knows that you can generate an ellipse with two nails and a string, but how do you place the nails and measure the string to generate an ellipse of a specific size? Here's how: Draw a long axis line down the center of the length of the top and a short axis line

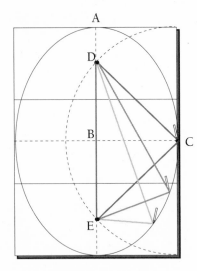

Draw an ellipse within any given rectangle by first bisecting it through both the long and short sides. Then set a compass to distance A, B, set one foot of the compass at point C and swing it in an arc to find points D and E. Now tap in nails at points C, D, and E and tie a string around the three nails. Pull out the nail at point C and put in a pencil to trace the ellipse perfectly within the rectangle.

This scratch stock finishes the convex part and, like its mate, is designed to gauge down from the top of the joint for accuracy.

[opposite]
Hinges for dropleaf rule joints have one leaf that is much longer than the other and screw holes that are countersunk on the side away from the barrel protrusion. The hinge needs to be inset so that the centerline of the barrel is at the center of the radius of the joint.

across the width. Adjust a pair of dividers to (or measure) half of the long axis. Now set one foot of the dividers on an outside end of the short axis and, scribing back with the other foot, mark the intersections of this arc with the long axis. Tack nails into both of these intersections and into the outside end of the short axis. Now tie a snug string around these three points and then pull out the nail on the short axis. Set a pencil within this loop of string and bring it around to trace a perfect ellipse within the rectangle. I have no idea why this works, but it sure does.

Saw the ellipse with a narrow-bladed saw that can manage the curves. Again, using a scratch stock is the easiest way to smooth the table-top edges to a neat round. Roughly round the edges with a spokeshave first and finish with the scratch stock.

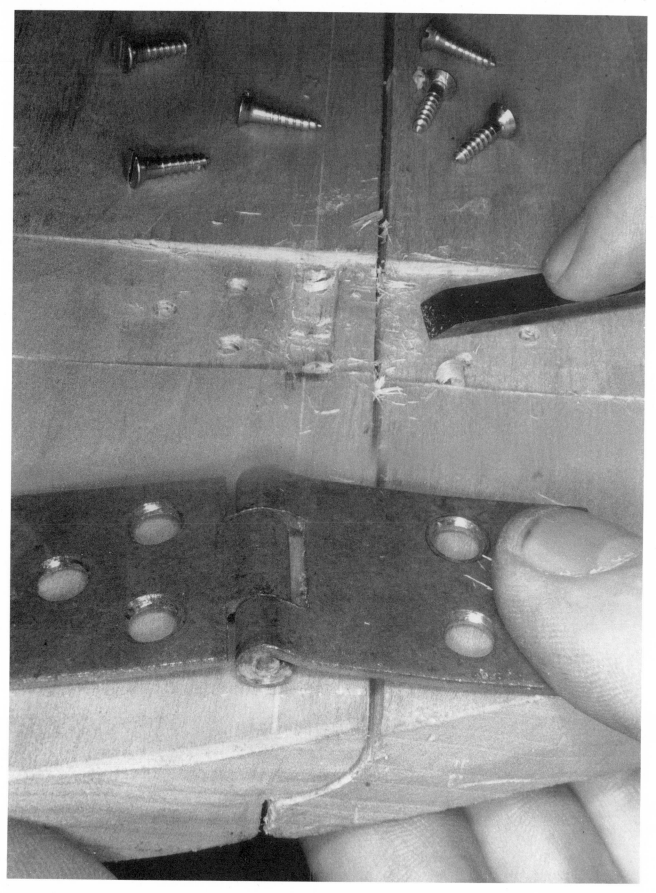

The bottom of the drawer slides into the groove from the back and should be glued only to the drawer front. This allows the drawer bottom to expand and contract harmlessly below the back with changes in humidity. Notice that the dovetails on the front (facing away) are "half-blind" and will not show through on the exposed face.

[opposite]
Clamp the sides together and scratch the length of the dovetails both around their ends and onto the end grain of the drawer front with one setting of the gauge.

Drawers

The little drawer in this table matches the convergence of the legs, but because it slopes on two sides only, you can dovetail it together in the same way as a normal drawer. The bottom fits in a groove plowed into the front and sides. If you cut the bottom so that its grain runs across the width of the drawer (and so that it extends under the back wall of the drawer), it will be able to expand and contract without bursting out the sides of the drawer. You must leave room for the expansion by making the back shorter than the front and sides. You could skip this measure on a drawer this narrow, but it is a good technique to know.

Carefully dimension your stock for the drawer. The sides and back are ⅜ inch thick and the front is ¾ inch. Most important, however, is that you saw the ends square and keep the thickness consistent. You will count on the consistent thickness of the sides to help you lay out the dovetails. Before dovetailing, plow the groove for the bottom around the front and sides. A plow plane makes this easy, but you can do a small job like this in a minute or two with a ¼-inch chisel. All you need to do is scratch the width of the groove into the surface before you chisel.

Laying out the Dovetails

Set your gauge for the thickness of the sides and back. With the fence of the gauge riding on the end grain, scratch this measure in all around the

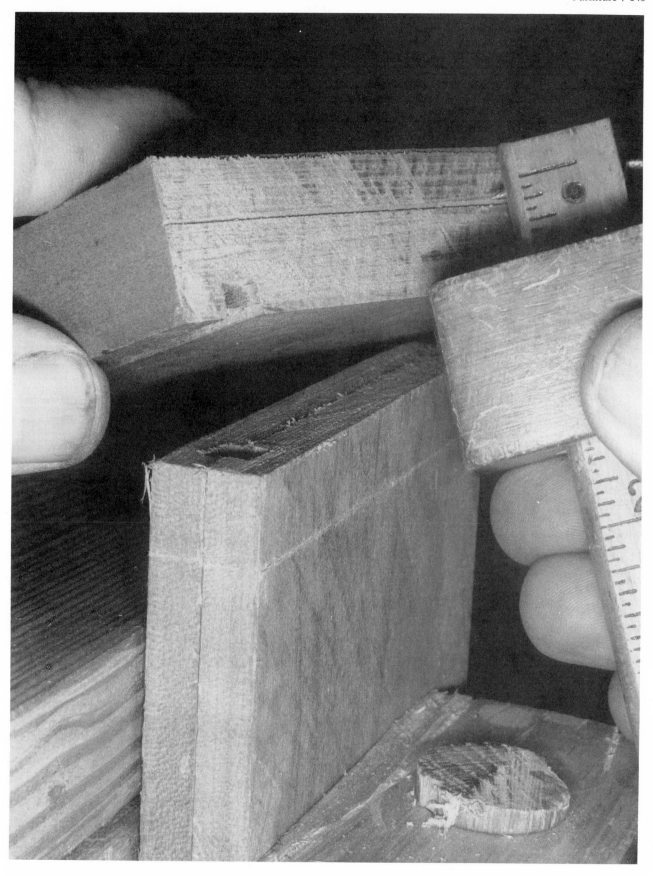

Make three saw cuts sloping down from right to left.

ends of the back, around the ends of the sides that will join to the back, and then just on the inside face of the drawer front.

The front dovetails are half-blind, which means they don't show through on the front of the drawer. Reset the gauge for about ⅓ of the thickness of the front and scratch this dimension in on the end grain of the front and around the ends of the sides that will join to it.

There are many ways to cut dovetail joints, but this is the best. First you make the saw cuts for the tails on the drawer sides, you then transfer these saw cuts to the front and back to guide the placement of the pins. (Pins are the wood that remains between the hollows cut for the tails.) Finally, you saw and chisel away the waste wood between the pins and tails and fit the perfect joints together.

Sawing the Tails

Clamp the two sides with their grooves together, placing the end that will join the drawer front upright in the vise. With a very fine saw, make three cuts down to the scratched line, sloping down from right to left. Now make three cuts sloping from left to right.

Include the groove within the dovetail defined by the outermost saw cut. These cuts should be square across the end grain and should slope at a bevel of about 1 inch of rise in 6 inches of run. Hold the sides tight together and reset them in the vise to saw the back tails.

Work the same way on the back end, but here, instead of including the groove for the bottom within the dovetails, you exclude it. Lay out the tails as if the inner edge of the groove were the outer edge of the board. The shorter drawer back will reach down only this far, giving the bottom room to expand and contract with the weather.

Next, make three cuts sloping down from left to right.

Transferring the Tails

As it now stands, you have sawn the dovetails on the sides but not removed any waste wood. It matters not if you cut entirely by eye. It matters not if the angles and placement of the tails are ruggedly individualistic. It matters not, because whatever pattern you established with these saw cuts on the sides will now be perfectly transferred to the front and back for a fast custom fit.

Clamp the drawer front upright in the vise with the groove facing away from you. Lay the appropriate drawer side with its saw-kerfed tails on the

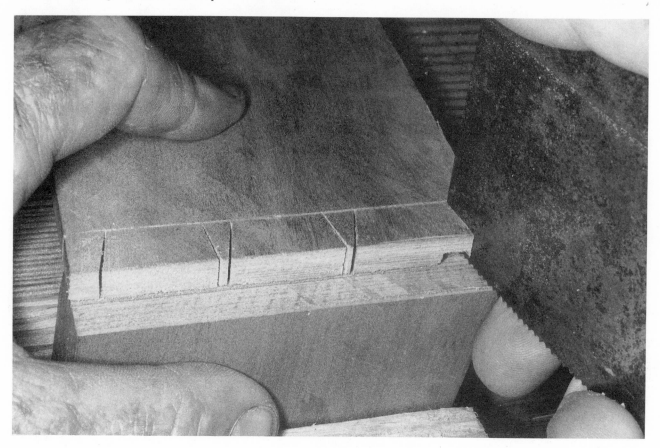

Set the drawer side where you want it to go into the front and transfer the dimensions by pulling back on the saw.

end grain of the front and hold it firmly in place. Align the side exactly as you wish it to fit into the front. Now set your saw blade in one of the kerfs in the drawer side and draw it back to leave a mark on the end grain of the drawer front. Press hard enough to make a mark, but not enough to cut into the wood. Don't let the drawer side move as you do the same to all the kerfs, transferring their locations precisely to the wood beneath it. Take the drawer side away and you should see the lines that will guide your saw through the next step.

Turn the drawer front in the vise so that the grooved side faces you. Depending on your level of confidence, you can either saw by eye or use a try square to place guidelines that drop down perpendicular from the edge. The important thing is to saw on the waste side of the lines. Mark the areas that you want to remove with X's and place the kerf so that it just touches the inner edge of the lines. In other words, leave the line. You can only saw the diagonals of the joints on the drawer front; the rest comes out with a chisel.

Lay the drawer front flat on the bench and either pare back or chop out the waste with your chisel. In paring back, you push down on the chisel and take off curls until you reach the scratched line. In chopping,

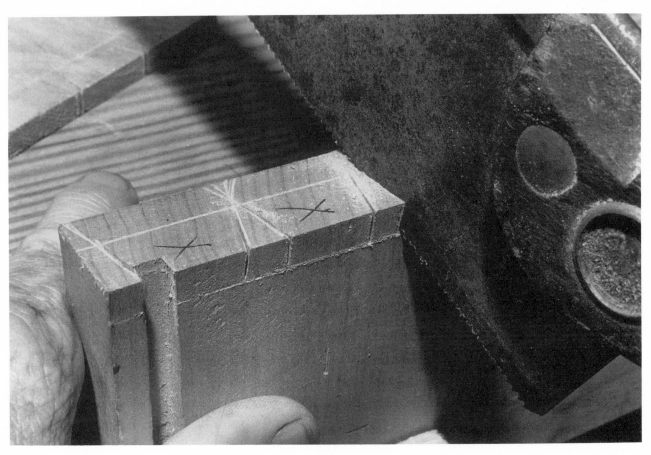

you drive in two cuts near the line to make a V. You then split back from the end grain and repeat until you reach the full depth. Chopping is the faster method, but try both. You will need your narrowest chisel to reach into the angle of the corners. A skew chisel (or even a small woodturning skew) is most handy. For the final trimming, you may find it convenient to clamp the work upright in the vise once again. Mark and cut all the work on the drawer front and back before you move on to complete the work on the sides.

Mark the pieces that you want to cut away with X's and saw diagonally down on the waste side of the line.

Finishing the Tails

Mark the areas that you want to remove with bold X marks. Saw off the corner pieces of the tails with your fine saw and most of the wood between the tails with a coping saw. You can also chop the wood from between the tails, but a coping saw makes quicker work of the job. Whether chopping or sawing, stay to the inside of the lines, leaving the finishing touches for the fine paring chisel. As your final cut before assembly, slightly bevel the inner corners of the tails to help them ease into their sockets.

Trying a dovetail joint together for fit once before gluing it violates the

Finish the sockets for the dovetails (the intervening pieces are called the pins) by paring back with a chisel. Notice how the groove for the drawer bottom is housed within the dovetail socket to the right.

same rule as flipping a pancake more than once—it exhibits a lack of confidence that old sourdoughs and young masters like to ridicule. On a practical note, though, repeated assembly of a joint will compress the wood, round the corners, loosen it, and make it weaker. If you have cut to the lines, the joint should tap together easily the first time. Set a board across the top and work your way back and forth, tapping with a hammer. Slip the bottom into place to hold the drawer square as the glue dries and stick another feather in your cap.

THE OLD KITCHEN TABLE

What a great axe! It's had two heads, seven handles,
and it's still going strong!
– ancient joke

I grew up convinced that the Pilgrims had their first Thanksgiving dinner on the same walnut tabletop where I ate my cornflakes. "Sure it's had some repairs," said my mother, "but this old table has been in our family since 1627." It was the hinges on the dropleaves that first made me suspect our cherished family tradition. Unless there was a hingemaker named STANLEY on the Mayflower, something was wrong with our table.

The Tree and the Trestle

With careful research (and a heavy dose of imagination), I have solved the mystery. Our walnut dropleaf table did begin in 1627—but as a pine trestle table.

This trestle table was 2 feet wide and 12 feet long, just enough room for family and friends. The two massive top planks were split from a pine log, smoothed with adz and plane, and then joined along their undersides with wooden dovetails. These dovetails, or "butterflies," only slightly resemble the dovetails used to join the corners of boxes and drawers. After the tabletop boards were jointed and glued, these bowtie-shaped pieces were set across the seam and their outlines carefully traced with a knife. Recesses were chiseled out and the dovetails were glued into place. They linked the planks with the strength of their long grain and the unbeatable holding power of opposing wedges.

The Drunkard and the Dropleaf

The table endured its first major improvement just after the American Revolution, at the hands of its fourth owner. Beset with flu and fever, the old soldier undertook the "two-hat cure." (He put his hat on the table and drank apple brandy until he saw two hats.) Unfortunately, while he was in his curative stupor, his candle burned through and ruined the tabletop.

Finish the dovetails on the sides by chiseling out the pieces between them. The missing part of the dovetail to the right is the end of the groove in the side.

And it all fits together perfectly.

The top had to be replaced, and the old soldier had just the right stuff for it—three big walnut boards that he had won in a horse race. Shortening the stretchers between the trestles, he remade the Puritan dining board into an oversized card table.

As often happens, the wood used by the old soldier was better than his workmanship. This discrepancy, coupled with the odd match of the walnut top and the pine trestle base, motivated the table's seventh owner to have it restored as a genuine "Early American table." The Centennial celebration of 1876 was fast approaching, and the local cabinetmaker was working overtime "restoring" such unfortunate antiques. He chopped up the pine trestle base for kindling and replaced it with a proper "colonial" one of carved walnut with knuckle-jointed legs.

Cutting the knuckle joints was easier than it looked. With chisels and planes, the cabinetmaker shaped the ends of the two boards into partial cylinders. He then cut away alternating sections from each cylinder to allow them to intermesh. Iron rods through the centers completed these wooden hinges. The length of the knuckle joints gave the essential stability to the swing-out legs that supported the dropleaves—dropleaves that he recut from the "old original" walnut top.

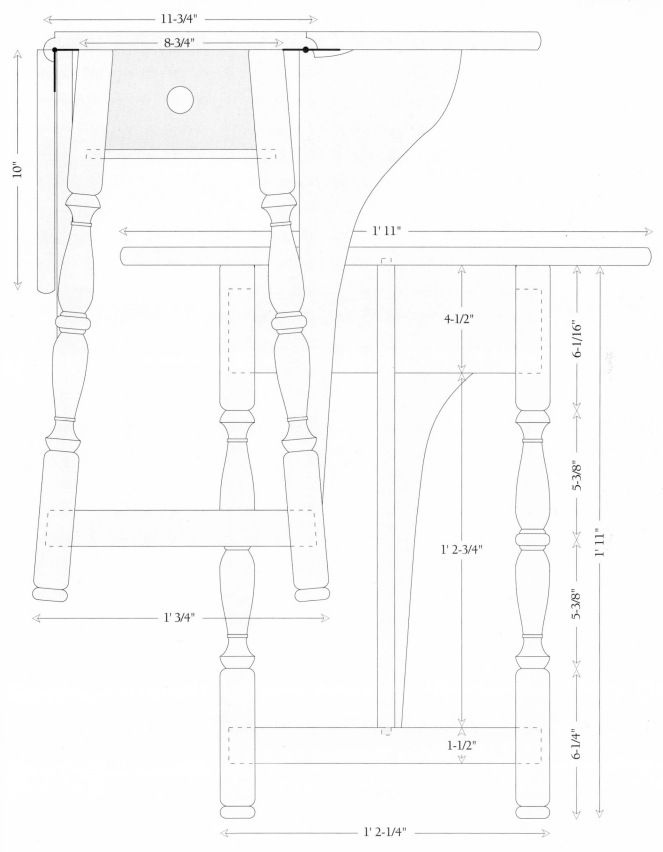

11-3/4"

8-3/4"

10"

1' 11"

4-1/2"

6-1/16"

1' 2-3/4"

5-3/8"

1' 11"

5-3/8"

1' 3/4"

1-1/2"

6-1/4"

1' 2-1/4"

Butterfly tavern table.

The revolving bookcase holds a lot of books in a small space.

The cabinetmaker rejoined the dropleaves with rule joints (so called because of their resemblance to an old folding ruler). These joints were ideal for dropleaves because any load on the leaf is supported by the main top. As he shaped the hollow and round elements of the rule joint with his two moulding planes, the cabinetmaker took serious pride in the knowledge that he was making a better Pilgrim table than the Pilgrims ever had.

Finally the table came down to me, with not a bit of the original wood remaining. I am still proud of it though; not everyone has a walnut table that began as a pine tree.

REVOLVING BOOKCASE

This revolving bookcase is great for keeping a lot of reference books handy by your desk. It uses turf more efficiently to hold more books while taking up less wall space than a conventional bookshelf. You can make this basic design in any size or shape. I made a three-tiered version in pine that is far too big and bulky. I will have to cut it down, but I am glad that I saw how it would look in pine before doing it in walnut.

Another reason for not making this bookcase too big is that the sheer *avoirdupois* of all those weighty tomes can put a mighty strain on the stoutest structure. The bookcase is built around four identically sized and

This dado plane is designed to cut grooves across the grain, such as for the shelves of this bookcase. The blade ahead of the main cutter has two nickers to score across the grain and ensure a splinter-free cut.

grooved vertical boards. These boards join vertically like four hands, each clasping the wrist of the adjoining arm to form a small rectangular tube for the pivot shaft between them. The intermediate, cross-grained grooves, or dadoes, support the shelves. The pivot shaft tenons into a base of half-lapped 2 by 4 stock. The whole structure is thus quite strong, but the entire load is carried by a steel point set into the top of the shaft. You may be pressing your luck if you try to spin the large-print edition of the OED on a steel pin.

Groovin'

Ordinary shelving boards, 11¼ by ¾, are the right size for the verticals. Cut four equal lengths that are as long as you want the bookcase tall. Use the double-toothed marking gauge to lay out a ¾-inch-wide groove 1½ inches in from one edge on each of the boards. Now, with plow plane, router plane, or chisel, cut these grooves ¼ inch deep. You can now put all four boards together to see how they form the hollow square. If your work is accurate and precise, the fourth board will have to slip in from the end. That is as it should be.

Take the boards apart again and stack them with the grooves all to the same side. Using a try square, mark the locations for the intermediate shelves (there may be one or two) on the edges of all four boards at once. Separate the boards and extend these lines across both faces of each board. Check to see that the lines are still aligned at the far edges of the boards and make corrections as necessary. Each pair of lines marks the width of a ¼-inch-deep groove to hold a shelf.

Because these grooves are dadoes, cut across the grain rather than going with the grain, they require a slightly different approach than the grooves that join the verticals. In long-grain grooving, you can just push the blade along without worrying (too much) about tearing along the edges. When going across the grain, however, you need to sever the fibers on either side of the groove before you can safely extract the wood in between. Dado planes made for this job have nippers on either side just ahead of the broad blade. With every pass, the nippers free the wood within the groove so it can be lifted without splintering. Alternatively, you can score the edges of the dado with a knife, cut them to their full depth with a saw, and take out the wood between the kerfs with a chisel or router plane.

Saw out the 9-inch by 11¼-inch shelves so that their end grain is on the narrower side and will thus be partially covered by the vertical slats. These measurements include an allowance ¼ inch longer and wider than the exposed dimensions to fit into the dadoes. These shelves can go into place only after the vertical boards have been put together. Before you finish joining the verticals, make a stout block that you can glue and screw into place near the top of the hollow interior column. This block needs a plate

[opposite]

The long grain grooves join the four vertical planks, forming a square tube at the center to house the pivot.

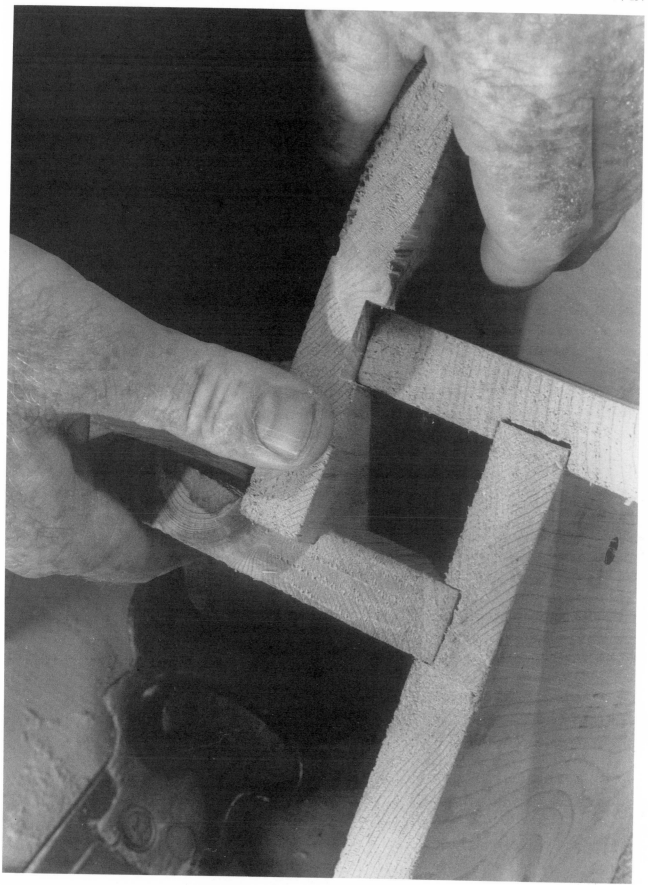

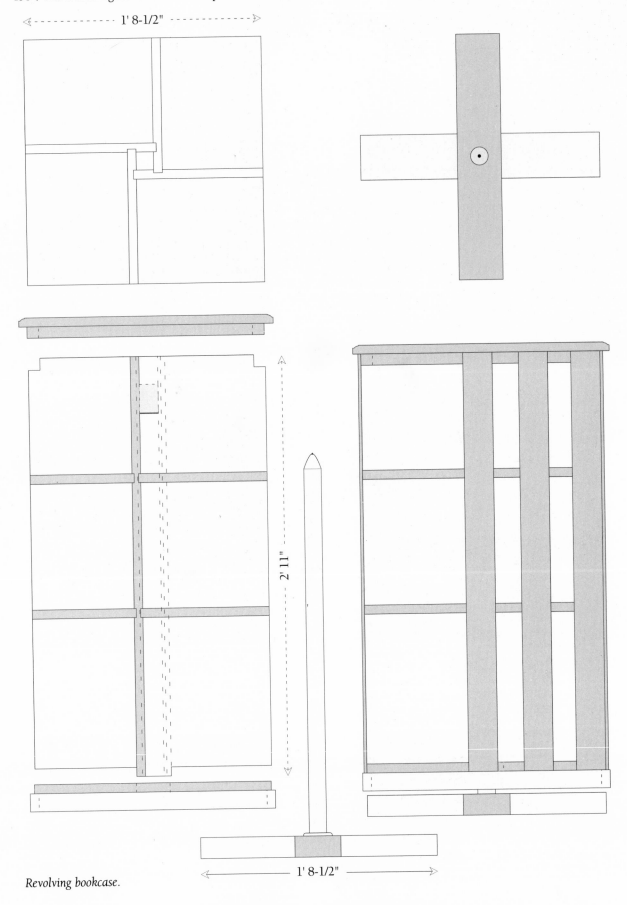

Revolving bookcase.

of scrap steel on its underside with a centered hollow to take the thrust of the pivot pin. Once a shelf is in position, you can nail or screw into it from the opposite side of the groove to hold it as the glue dries. Obviously, you can't nail the last shelf unless you have staggered the height of the shelves on alternating sides (which is not a bad idea).

Glue up the top and bottom of the bookcase, two flat boards and a rectangular frame to nail the side slats to. These slats express most of the visible style of the case. Modern designs often use dowels on the sides, but the old, cheap, turn-of-the-century bookcases are sided with ¼-inch by 2-inch oak slats.

The legs are half-lapped together and bored to hold the pivot.

Adirondack chairs on Bikini Island, waiting for the bomb, 1951.

The base is simply a cross made by half-lapping two lengths of 2 by 4 stock. The joint will come out perfectly if you lay out the depth of the half-lap by gauging halfway down from the top face of both pieces. If you cut down to this line on one piece, and up to this line on the other, they can't help but be right when you put them together. Bore a 1½-inch hole through the center of the intersection of the two pieces for the base of the shaft. Arm the end of the shaft with a long steel screw and file the end off to a point. The long thread, screwed into the end grain of the shaft, should keep the screw from being forced deeper into the end grain by the load of books.

COUNTRY COMFORT—ADIRONDACK CHAIR

Adirondack chairs, the most modern, cut-and-dried design of all chairs, have become mighty popular in recent years. They are quick and cheap to build, and you can set a drink on the flat arms. You hear all kinds of stories about their invention. Some are probably true, but I believe they evolved on the worksite. Whenever we have a pause in the work, and there is an empty wooden wheelbarrow about, it immediately becomes someone's armchair on the grass. To turn that into a real chair, all that you need are

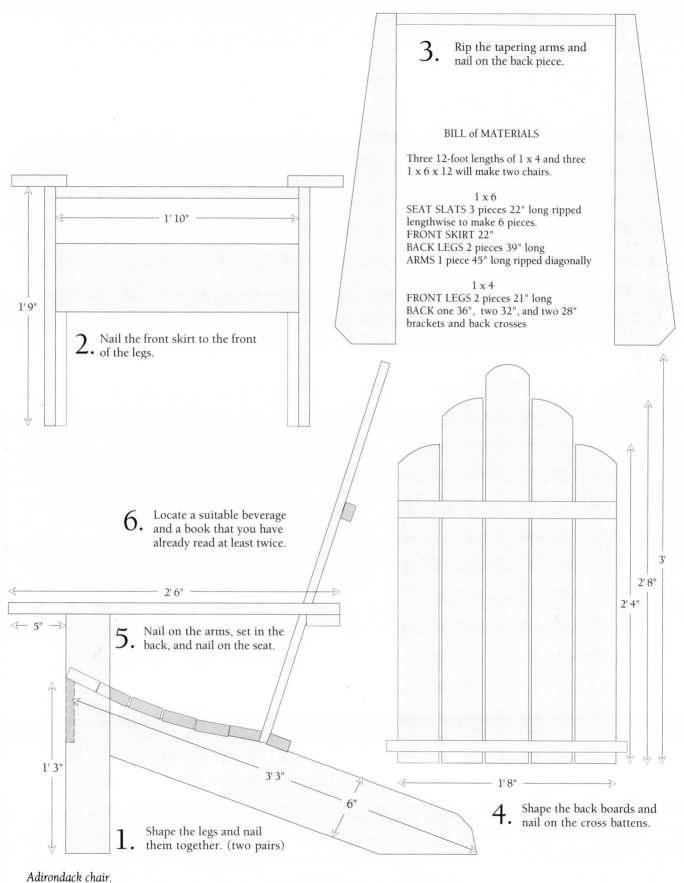

3. Rip the tapering arms and nail on the back piece.

BILL of MATERIALS

Three 12-foot lengths of 1 x 4 and three 1 x 6 x 12 will make two chairs.

1 x 6
SEAT SLATS 3 pieces 22" long ripped lengthwise to make 6 pieces.
FRONT SKIRT 22"
BACK LEGS 2 pieces 39" long
ARMS 1 piece 45" long ripped diagonally

1 x 4
FRONT LEGS 2 pieces 21" long
BACK one 36", two 32", and two 28"
brackets and back crosses

1' 10"

1' 9"

2. Nail the front skirt to the front of the legs.

6. Locate a suitable beverage and a book that you have already read at least twice.

2' 6"

5"

5. Nail on the arms, set in the back, and nail on the seat.

1' 3"

3' 3"

6"

1. Shape the legs and nail them together. (two pairs)

3'

2' 8"

2' 4"

1' 8"

4. Shape the back boards and nail on the cross battens.

Adirondack chair.

the boards, some nails, a hammer, and a saw. During the Great Depression, many an out-of-work handyman turned to making these chairs.

Saw out the two long pieces for the legs and the two shorter uprights. You can quickly chop and smooth the curved part with a hatchet and spoke shave. Nail them together and stand the two pairs beside each other with the uprights facing to the outside. Nail the front skirt to the end grain of the long legs and then nail through the uprights into the end grain of the skirt. These nails will be pretty close to the edge of the uprights, so take care to blunt the points of the nails by tapping them with the hammer so that they will punch through rather than wedging the wood into a split. A slight error will not be as readily apparent if the front skirt is inset by a quarter-inch. You can usually turn out neat-looking work faster if you deliberately offset pieces at a junction rather than trying for a flush match.

Bevel the top corners of the seat slats with a plane before nailing them on. Nail the front slat first, then the back slat, and then fill in the middle, spacing evenly.

The arms are basically a big, squared-off U shape that you nail together and then nail to the tops of the upright legs. You can make the arms from a single board sawn in half diagonally. You will have two little triangles left over from this sawing, and these can be nailed under the front arms as support brackets.

The back may be made flat or curved, plain or with heart-shaped cut-outs, as you wish. (Remember, if you are in business, that there are people out there that will buy *anything* with a heart shape on it.) The back part of the arm assembly will become the middle back support, so if you are planning a curved back, this piece should be curved as well. Nail the back slats together and drop the whole rig into place within the U of the arms and catching behind the last slat of the seat. You may wish to sit in the un-nailed chair and refine the angle of the back by moving the arm assembly back and forth. When you're happy with the feel of it, nail it down, carry the chair to a good spot, and fix yourself a mint julep.

THE CARVER'S SON

Anthony Merano's son took little interest in his father's work, which was just the way the old man wanted it. He had come to America in 1926 as a penniless apprentice woodcarver from northern Italy. He worked hard and was soon supplying fine architectural carving to builders throughout the country. Although he was the fourth generation of woodcarvers in his family, he thought there would be little demand for old-fashioned wood-carvers in space-age America. That is why he sent his only son to the best schools to study aerospace engineering, a career for the future.

When the old man developed heart trouble, he moved in with his son's family. Although he had had to give up his carving business, people kept on calling for his work. Father and son shared the same name, and it soon became a family joke that callers for Anthony Merano were asked if they wanted "the woodcarver" or "the rocket scientist."

The joke continued until the big slump hit the aerospace industry, and the middle-aged Anthony Merano, Jr., was laid off. He tried to find new work, but he simply could not compete with the younger people trained in the latest technology. His despair deepened daily, and when his father died, the son's spirits plummeted.

Sitting on the bottom steps of the cellar one afternoon, pondering which items to unload at yet another yard sale, Anthony Merano's gaze fixed on his father's tool chest. The key was fastened to the lid with masking tape. He pulled it free and unlocked the chest. Lifting the lid, he beheld a sight no more comprehensible to him than the inner workings of a typewriter. There must have been a hundred tool handles poking up from their racks.

He pulled out a gouge and a surprisingly heavy mallet of chocolate-and-butterscotch-colored wood. They felt good in his hands. Striking them together in the air, he heard the sound that had filled so much of his childhood, and he missed his father.

Glancing into the box, Merano noticed bundles of wooden blocks, carefully bound together with torn strips of cloth. He set the tools back down, untied one of the sets of variously carved blocks, and set them out on his knees. There were six blocks in this set, each measuring 6 inches square and 1 inch thick. He looked at the two rows for a long minute and then began to laugh.

He had wondered what was going on down in the cellar when he heard his father working there during those last few weeks. The answer lay before him. Here, in six sequential steps, were the techniques for carving a floral rosette. The other bundles held the designs for mouldings, panels, and the full range of his father's work. That night he just looked, but in the weeks and months that followed, he put everything he had into learning the lessons his father had prepared for him.

The following day, he cleared off his father's carving bench, laid out the series of rosette blocks, and tried to match the tools to the work. The first block had the flower penciled upon it with flawless sweeps of the compass. On the second block, the penciled design was outlined with knife cuts and a narrow channel. He searched in the chest until he found a tool that matched the channel.

With the first block clamped in the vise, he set the veiner (he had learned the names from a tool catalog) on the basswood block. He guided the tool around the curve of a petal, daring to take only the shallowest cut. The tool took off on its own, tracking into the grain and through the outline of an adjoining petal. He backed off and took a deeper, more forceful cut. This time the edge of the veiner caught under the grain and tore out a splinter to one side.

He stopped again and analyzed the problem. Parts of each curve led the tool with the grain, and parts led the tool against the grain. But whichever way he went, one side or the other of the gouge was always cutting against the grain. He tried to remember how his father had worked. He removed the block from the vise and held it pressed against a peg in the bench top. Now he could quickly turn the block to let him approach the cut from the best angle to the grain. He finished the outlining within the hour, anxious to copy the next block, in which his father had struck the channels with deep incisions.

In this step, each portion of each curve had been deepened by striking down with the gouge that most closely matched the curvature at that point. This part of the work went fast, and Merano wondered if he could skip the first step. He tried tapping in without the initial valley cut, but the surface chipped to the side. Each step had its purpose.

The fourth block was radically different from the first three. On this one, his father had carved away the background with long strokes of the gouge. Merano copied the gougework, first using a gouge that left round channels in the wood. He discovered how the shallowly curved, fishtail-shaped gouge was able to turn into corners and flow across the ridges, slicing the backgrounds flat.

By that evening, he had copied the roughly shaped hollows of the wooden petals on the fifth block and had added much of the detailing that made the sixth block come to life. He thought he had carved long enough that he could finish the rosette with sandpaper. Finding none in the chest, he retrieved a sheet from his wife's refinishing supplies. Wrapping the paper around his fingers to get in the hollows, he rubbed and rubbed all over, working by feel and scarcely looking at the work. Finally he held it up to the light. All the detail that gave interest to the piece had melted away. He knew he had made a mistake, but he didn't care. He felt great.

Within the year Anthony Merano was carving reasonably well. He still had a long way to go in judging proportion and working with any speed. But he was working, he was good, and he was getting better. His confidence grew. The phone rang. "Anthony Merano," he answered. "Oh, hello," came the voice on the other end. "I'm sorry, is this the rocket scientist or the woodcarver?"

He didn't hesitate for a second.

5 Amusements

Q: How did you happen to begin this work?

A: I don't exactly know—unless to please some child.

– from Allen Eaton, *Handicrafts of the Southern Highlands*, 1937

[overleaf]
Making things together is the most fun of all. Eleanor and I are working on the little rocking horse.

THE TOYMAKER

Our ancestors probably saw a bit of toymaking as a rare and welcome break from the harsher chores of American frontier life. Forgetting the farm for a moment, a parent might make a hobbyhorse from a stick and a plank or joint together a dancing man of contrasting poplar and walnut. Even at work, there could be time for the children. A cooper might spare one of the hickory bands from a hogshead so that his daughter could have a hoop to roll about. A turner might easily make a spinning top for his son from a scrap of beech. Parents have always been toymakers—and so have children, who can turn a block of wood into a car or a castle in no time.

Toymaking can be a business, too. The Tower Guild, an early company founded in Massachusetts in the 1830s, was actually a sales cooperative of local independent craftsmen. Working at home or in tiny shops, using glue pots, hammers, and nails, guild members assembled doll furniture and mechanical "sand toys." These sand toys used sand flowing from a hopper to turn a paddle wheel that drove the little action figures.

As with many trades in early America, the whole family might work together to make toys. One such family, the Herders, worked as a coordinated team of specialists. A visitor to their home found them gathered around a table like a scene from Santa's workshop, "carving little wooden horses and doing it very quickly." The oldest boy cut out the blocks and roughly shaped them before before passing them to the father, who refined the outline. Next the horse passed to the mother, who "quickly and neatly separated the hind legs, smoothed and shaped them, cut down the front legs until they were slender and shapely, modeled the ears, the nose, the neck, until the little horse, no larger than your hand, looked quite alive." Finally, she passed the horse to the youngest son, who "made some long, fine lines to represent the mane."

This family was probably carving in soft white pine, the favorite wood of the toymaker. Tougher woods could be used, but, as one toymaker recalled in 1850, only when they were specially treated: "To make the toys we boil the wood—green and soft, though sometimes dry; alder, willow, birch, poplar or ash are used. When the wood has been boiled, the toy is cut with a knife, and fixed together with glue, then painted."

The Ring of Beasts

Even with the entire family at work on the softest wood, hand carving every little horse and cow can simply take too long to be profitable. One of the most ingenious techniques for the quantity production of little animals is that of the turned ring. The toymaker begins by cutting the profile of a single animal into the periphery of a wooden disc as it spins in the lathe. When this disc is later sawn radially into dozens of narrow pie-slices, each

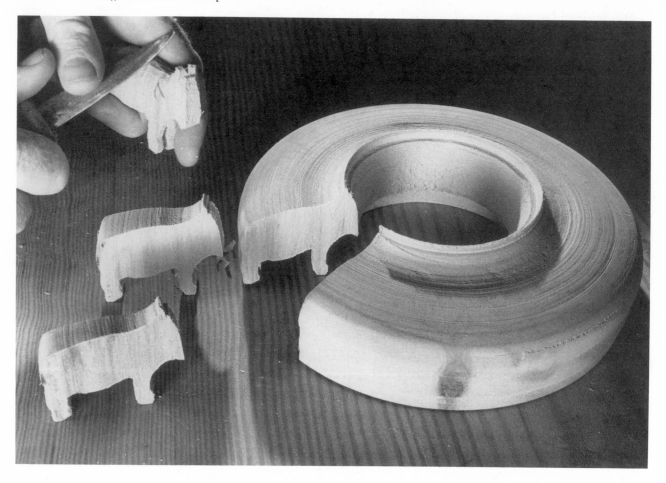

The ring of beasts. Turning an animal shape into the circumference of a wooden disk allows you to saw out individual animals like pieces of pie. The slices are ready to whittle into finished beasts.

slice will be a perfect little animal-blank, ready for the finishing carving. You can readily pick out animals produced by this method, because they will invariably taper toward one end or the other. Most animals are turned with their heads facing the center of the ring and thus are larger in their hindquarters. Lions and tigers, however, face out to make them bigger on their biting ends.

Two by Two

All of these wooden animals had to have a home. For many of them, it was inside one of the few toys that nineteenth-century parents considered appropriate for Sunday play—the Noah's Ark. In Charles Dickens's story "The Cricket on the Hearth," toymaker Caleb Plummer crafted Noah's Arks "in which the Birds and Beasts were an uncommonly tight fit. . . . By a bold poetical license, most of these Noah's Arks had knockers on the doors; inconsistent appendages, perhaps, as suggestive of morning callers and a postman, yet a pleasant finish to the outside of the building." The Noah's Ark met with parental approval in part because it was an "educational toy" and was clearly "good for the children."

Woodworkers traditionally have helped their children to learn the trade by providing them with tools of their own. An old carpenter once recalled that his father "always encouraged us to take an interest in the work and even purchased a small pedal lathe which he allowed us to use. For this he gave us oddments of hard beech, which we turned into whiptops and sold to other village boys at a halfpenny each."

Lathes are fun to use, but a powerful one is definitely not a toy, as this same boy soon discovered: "Later on we aspired to the turning of a large set of ninepins and balls. For this we used the large lathe and a stalwart companion was enlisted to turn the six-foot driving wheel for us. The wood was hard, and through some cause unknown, when I applied the gouge, I suddenly found my hand between the 'rest' and the rapidly turning wood. Before my companion succeeded in stopping the wheel, the wood had ground the skin from the front of my four fingers."

Busy people never have more right to pride than when they have made something for a child or when they have helped the next generation of toy-makers along. I met a boy the other day, fourteen years old, who has been badly bitten by the hand-tool woodworking bug. His little shop would be the envy of any man of ample means, yet his lathes, his dozens of planes, his tool chests—all were paid for by himself. His parents had given him a treadle jigsaw for his thirteenth birthday. So how did he pay for the rest of his tools? By making and selling wooden toys.

Chris in the little shop that he built, paid for, and equipped by himself.

TOYS

Jacob's Ladder

Endlessly falling but never moving. I have seen these things all my days and I still don't know how they work. I know how to make them work just right. I know where to buy the bias tape. I know how tedious the nailing is. But when they work, they seem to operate on another plane of logic and reason.

Use heavy wood—light, soft pine or poplar may not have enough mass to fall and clack with conviction. The ribbon is sold as bias binding tape and is available in most any width and color. Tiny brass brads will hold the tape to the ends. You can easily assemble the pieces by stacking them up like a layer cake. Nail two ribbons to one end of the first block and one ribbon to the other end. Bring these ribbons up across the face of the block and lay the second block atop them. Pass the ribbons back across this face, then repeat until all the blocks are laid up in the ribbons like a Austrian torte. Keep the ribbons flat, but do not stretch them. A little slack is good. Turn the assembled blocks on their ends and nail the ribbons where they pass over the ends. It's done.

Stack the tiles with the ribbons crossing between them and tack them on the ends.

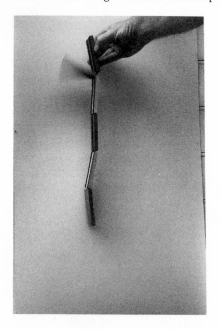

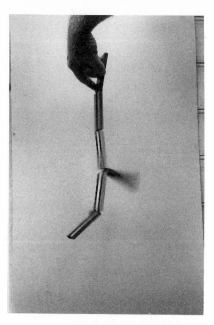

The Jacob's ladder. Endlessly falling but never moving, easy to make, hard to figure.

Snake Box

Slide back the lid and a little snake pops out and bites your finger. It's not the deadly treasure box from Poe's "The Gold Bug," but it can give someone quite a start. I have yet to discover the origin of this little trick box. They were made in Germany (one-time toymaker to the world) around the turn of the century, and I have also seen them carved from stone in African versions. Cigar-box wood is ideal for this sort of work, but it is almost extinct. The lid slides in grooves that you can make with a saw or chisel. Make the snake out of heavy-gauge, insulated copper wire with a wooden head. Its motion relative to the lid is similar to the action of a piano. The surprise works because the snake moves at a much higher velocity than the lid. The cord wraps closely around the axle so that ½ inch of travel by the lid produces 4 inches of travel by the snake head. It's the same principle of leverage that causes the crank handle on a well windlass to knock you silly when the bucket falls back down the well.

Exploding Bank

The exploding bank is obviously pretty modern in that it engages the mechanics of a mousetrap to do its dirty deed. A coin dropping through the slot hits the catch and releases the spring. Three of the walls must have protruding pins to engage the spring trap as it rises. The top and bottom need grooves to hold the walls together loosely, ready for demolition. The mousetrap can hurt unwary fingers, so you may wish to add a safety chain to stop it in the vertical position. Some have suggested that the exploding bank works best when it is inscribed with "Help restore St. Bede's" and left in the church on a table by the leaflets, but you did not hear that from me.

Noveltails

Now, you know about dovetails: one keystone-shaped piece fits into a corresponding hollow. The keystone shape keeps the joint from pulling apart in one direction, but it can always come apart in the same direction as it went together. Here are two classic puzzlers that look as though they are dovetailed in two directions and apparently will not come apart. Even more puzzling, how did they go together?

The pieces move on the diagonal. The first puzzler is the dovetail that joins two square sections of wood end to end so that it seems the dovetails are on all four faces, at right angles to each other. Actually, there are just two long dovetails that sit parallel to one another and diagonal to the square faces. Square the two pieces of wood carefully to ensure that they match. Scribe the dovetails on all four faces and connect adjoining corners with diagonal lines across the end grain. Saw and chisel the wood

Oh, it's that snake-in-the-box again!
Slide back on the lid and it pulls a thread
wound around the axle of the snake,
which pops up and bites you.

Oh, it's that exploding bank! I hate that!

Impossible dovetails! How can you dovetail from converging right angles? How did they go together? How do they come apart?

Fooled again—it's those darned diagonals!

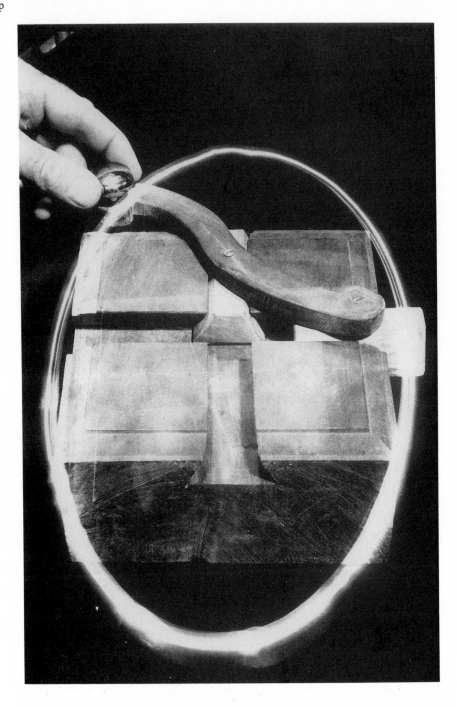

The do-nothing machine, or smoke grinder, is both a dumb gag and a way to generate an ellipse with sliding dovetails.

away, working slowly down to a snug fit. The irritating line of dumb tricks continues.

The single impossible dovetailed T joint is often used in making puzzle mallets. Again, the dovetail seems impossible because we think of it as being in the same plane as the timbers. This is easier to see in the picture than to explain. Aside from mallets, I have seen this joint used as the base of a reading stand in the schoolhouse on an old Virginia plantation. I suppose it teaches us that all is not exactly as it seems.

The final expression of the dovetail puzzle is more interactive but just

as useless. Known as the smoke grinder or the do-nothing machine, it consists of a thick plank with crossed dovetail grooves. Two dovetail keys fit loosely in these grooves and move at cross purposes as you propel them with the crank arm. The curious thing about this arrangement is that as the dovetail keys dart back and forth at right angles to one another, the crank handle describes an ellipse. By varying the attachment points of the keys to the handles, you can generate any size ellipse you desire. This is a common cabinetmaker's tool, a geometrical gem, and an idiot's delight in one.

I couldn't figure this one out at all.

The Quarter in the Block

Now for one that completely baffled me. A distant cousin showed me a single block of wood that had tiny windows in either side, through which you could look and see a quarter inside the block—with no possible way that it could have gotten in there. It was made by my great-uncle when he was a boy in 1887. Try as I might, I could not find any seam or break in the block. The only hint I was given was that my great-uncle did not work alone, and that his partner worked three years on the project and was killed upon its completion.

Give up? It was made with a living tree and an auger. Sometimes called cottonwood trees, they are *Paulownia tomentosas* or Princess trees to most people, and they grow fast. My great-uncle bored a hole in the side of a living tree, placed the quarter in the hole, and waited for the wood to close up around it. Chopping the block from the tree, he whittled it down to the piece I later saw. By far the most remarkable facet of this accomplishment is the ability to keep your mouth shut about it for three years as the tree grows up.

Chessboard

Chessboards are fun to make, which is reason enough to do it. They are also a rewarding introduction to the systematic process for young workers. True up and glue together alternating cutoffs of contrasting wood into a large sandwich. The end grain of these cutoffs must face the broad surface of the sandwich just as if you were making a butcher's block. Plane these end-grain faces true and then saw slices off the end to free a row of alternating tablets. By flipping the direction of the slices as you glue them down to the baseboard you will generate the ancient table of combat. Your move.

Music Mill from Bali

Claire Mehalic, old friend and world traveler, discovered these musical whirligigs on the island of Bali in the South Pacific and brought one to me. As the wind turns the propeller, bamboo "bonkers" strike bamboo bars to play music, and a crank animates a traditional Balinese dancer. I am delighted with it, not only for its considerable charm, but for the lessons to be learned from its making. It is of bamboo, a grass with a strong message for the woodworker. Traditional woodworkers must understand and work with the grain of their material. Bamboo brings this lesson home in spades, rewarding strict compliance with the rules of its grain.

One bamboo pole will give you enough stuff to make a score of these whirligigs, but avoid punky bamboo that has started to go soft. Although

[opposite]

You can make a chessboard by gluing up blocks of contrasting wood and then sawing it into strips that you then glue in alternate directions to a baseboard. Notice that the "mother block" has to be glued up with the end grain facing the broad surface like a butcher's block to ensure that the grain is correct in the slices.

The bamboo whirlygig from Bali. The "bonkers" bonk the bamboo tablets to make music as the lady dances.

bamboo has become so well established in places that it is considered a pest, some people are protective of their bamboo groves. Other groves have all but become public domain where folks have cut bamboo fishing poles for generations. If you have any doubt, ask before you help yourself. Go with the grain.

The base pole on my music mill (they can be any size) is about 1 inch in diameter and about 14 inches long. If you can find a piece with nodes at this spacing, so much the better. Otherwise, you can carve a wooden block that fits in one end to nail the uprights to. Saw with the finest-toothed saw you have. You can make a cleaner saw cut by slowly rolling the bamboo away from you as you go, so that you are always sawing through the near wall of the cylinder.

The base pole supports four uprights, three flat and one round. Two flat ones are simply nailed to either end, the third fits into a slot in the top side, and the round upright pivot pole passes entirely through the diameter. Make the hole for the pivot pole through the base pole using a sharp knife. Here is where you will learn that you can't just twist the knife into the bamboo without splitting and ruining it. Think of the grain as the north-south axis through a globe. To keep from cutting against the grain, you must always cut from a pole to the equator, but never from the equator to a pole. Thus, you work the knife in four quadrants; the knife can cut in the same direction only in the quadrants diagonally across from each other. (You use the same principle in spindle turning when you cut from the large diameter to the small.)

The base pole also needs four rectangular slots in it: one to hold an upright, the others to open resonating chambers that will amplify the sound.

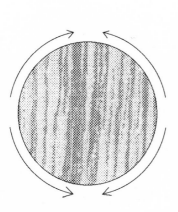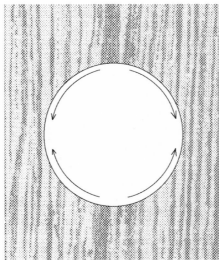

Here you can turn the roundness and hollow-osity of the bamboo to your advantage. Simply saw two parallel cuts across the grain and pop out the wood in between with your knife.

The uprights hold the drive shaft, which passes through a hole in each of them. Lay out the three flat uprights and the pivot pole together to ensure that all four holes will be in alignment. Split the three flat uprights from a 6-inch length of the largest-diameter bamboo that you have. This will give you slightly rounded pieces that you can flatten by drawing them back across your knee as you hold the knife against them. Trim their tops to little finials. You will find that the same principles apply here as when felling a tree. The knife cuts easily when the shaving has a place to go, but a straight-in cut is difficult, because the wood can't get out of the way to let the blade enter.

Each upright also has a rectangular mortice above the pivot hole to take the top beam. With a narrow chisel, you can make this mortice as you would any other. Rock the chisel down into the bamboo with the blade at right angles to the grain. When you have punched through the grain at either end of the opening, you can pry out the wood in between. If you turn the chisel to run with the grain, the piece will split. To make the slot in the end of the round pivot pole, cut a nick across the grain at the base of where you want the slot and split back from the end down to that point.

Nail two of the flat uprights onto the ends of the base pole and fit one down into its slot. Even the tiny nails that join these pieces can easily split the bamboo. You can prevent this by making a tiny nick with two cuts of your knife across the grain at the point where the nail goes in. Make sure that all the axle holes are aligned. Although this Balinese piece is nailed

On inside hollows and outside rounds, going with the grain means cutting in four quadrants. When you make a hole in bamboo with a knife, you need to cut the four strokes with the grain or risk splitting the piece.

[left]

The bonkers on the axle. Notice how the bonker arms have been nicked prior to being nailed to keep the piece from splitting.

[right]

The propeller attaches to the main shaft with a tiny mortice and tenon. The shaft is thick where it enters the first upright to act as a thrust bearing.

together, nails were pretty scarce in other parts of the South Pacific in the early days. When the HMS *Bounty* was in the neighborhood in 1789, the Polynesian women would swim beneath the ship and pull the nails out of its bottom.

Split bamboo will often warp, but you overcome that tendency when you join two split pieces into a T-beam to span the mortices through the tops of the uprights. Split out the long piece and shave it down to fit. Once it is in place, bend it if necessary to bring the four axle holes into alignment and nail on the top pieces to cross the T.

The drive shaft has to be the longest piece of all. Split it out and shave it down by pulling it into a knife blade held over your knee. Leave an inch on one end fat to provide a thrust bearing, and whittle a little tenon on the tip to join to the propeller. Whittle the propeller from another split piece of bamboo and cut a mortice in the middle to fit onto the shaft. Snip the blades from coffee can lids, set them into splits made on the ends of the propeller, and nail through both tin and bamboo to secure them.

Before you can put the shaft into place, you need to finish the "bonker arms" and "bonkers." Each bonker arm is a short length of bamboo with a transverse hole for the shaft through one end and a slot for the bonkers on the other end. Whittle the bonkers from the hardest bamboo and fit them so that they will drop and bonk the bars beneath them. These bars need to be made from very dense pieces of bamboo. Fasten them by loose nails with soft rubber washers beneath to let them sing. Tune the three bars to different notes by shaving them down and make multiple bonkers to play your song.

Finally, fit the dancer onto the end. On the tail end of the shaft, whittle a tiny tenon to hold an itsy-bitsy crank. Press a little nail into one end of the crank and attach a stiff wire upward to animate the dancing figure. Set the music and dance in the garden wind.

The dancing lady is pivoted at her navel and runs on a crank.

ROCKING HORSE

It's the horse foaled from an acorn, or, in this case, a pinecone. We discovered this little rocking horse in the corner of a café in Franconia, Germany. It was an antique and had been put out to pasture with a message on its back reading, "Please don't ride me, my back is already weak." Eleanor (who is nine) helped me make a copy of it. Shaving with drawknife and spokeshave are among her favorite activities, and I often have to stop work to pick out another piece of wood for her to work on. She is careful with the sharp tools, and I trust her with just about everything—except picking out wood that can be shaved just for the sake of shaving.

This is an excellent item for tuning the eye of a beginner for form and proportion. This horse has considerable integrity and personality. That's not due just to the simplicity of the design alone, (just nine pieces of wood from head to tail); it also has just a little bit of the dynamism of the galloping horse of Kansu.

Wood

This simple horse requires simple, stout wood. The finer the grain, the better and smoother the finished horse will be. The tail is fragile in that it must be cross-grained at some point, so use the strongest stock you can find. Walnut may be an interesting choice for the rockers, as it is reputed to be the one wood that will not move across the floor as you rock. Except for the rockers, which are possibly easier to make from sawn boards, you can easily split all the pieces for the horse from a good log.

For the head and legs, you must saw, split, or find planks about 1¾ inches thick. Trace the outline of the legs on the surface and saw them out with a bow or turning saw. As with all the parts, leave the edges square until the joints have been cut and fitted. Because the legs splay out to the sides as well as to the ends, you will need two settings on the bevel for the shoulders of the tenons that join the legs to the body. Lay out the tenons as follows:

The horse that foaled of an acorn.

1. Inscribe the side-splay angle on one edge of the legs.
2. From this line, inscribe the end-splay angle on the two broad faces of each leg.
3. Connect these last two lines across the remaining edge. The bevel should show the same angle on opposing faces.

You can lay out the inch-thick tenon and the width of the mortice in the 4-by-4 torso of the horse with a double-toothed morticing gauge. Remember that the surface opening of the mortice is an oblique slice of an inch-wide mortice and will, in this perspective, be wider than 1 inch. Reset your gauge after you lay out the tenons in the way described earlier for the legs of the folding lathe. If you prepare the mortice by boring 1-inch

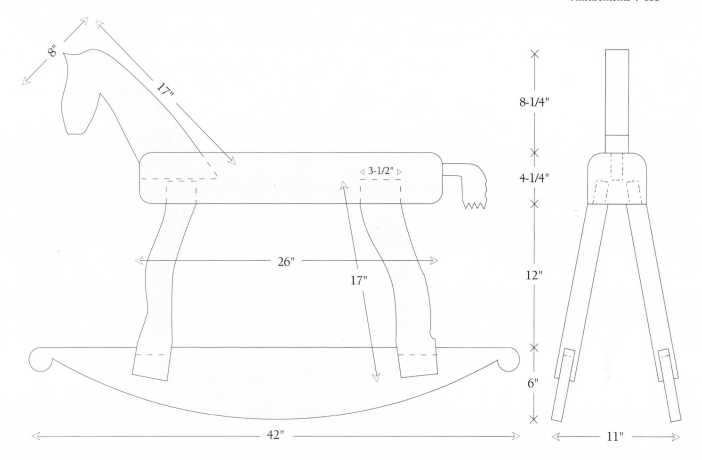

The rocking horse.

auger holes at the proper angle, the width of the opening will be correct. Use the bevel or the completed leg as a guide for angling the auger as you bore. Chisel the first of the joints to fit, drive the leg home, and use it to eyeball-guide the angles for the remaining three legs. Finally, when all the legs are as they should be, kerf in the shoulders to ensure a seamless juncture.

When the legs are in place, set the sawn-out rockers upon them and draw the lines for the bridle joints. On the legs, you need to mark the depth of the joints on the sides and the width of the joints on the end grain. The rockers, too, need notches atop them to further secure the joint, so mark their sizes and locations as well. You can easily cut the bridle joints in the legs by boring through with an auger and then sawing down the sides to remove the waste.

Saw out the head and make its mortice and tenon with an undercut to keep it from pushing off to the front. Secure it from pulling out backward by pinning it through the body. Finally, the tail goes directly into a hole drilled into the end. The fun part for the children—more fun than riding the horse—is the overall smoothing and blending of the angular parts with the spokeshave and sandpaper.

THE BOATBUILDERS

The manner of makinge their boates in Virginia is verye wonderfull.
– *Thomas Hariot,* Report of the New Found Land of Virginia, *1588*

For thousands of years, Native Americans harvested the bounty of the Chesapeake, making their boats from trees felled along its shores. Their tools were fire and seashells; their method, "somtymes burninge and some-tymes scrapinge." When the English came to the bay, many ridiculed the natives' bevel-ended "canowes," some even resorting to doggerel:

> The Indians call this Watry Waggon
> Canoo, a Vessel none can brag on;
> Cut from a Popular-tree or Pine
> And fashion'd like a Trough for Swine.

At the same time, though, they could not fail to notice that one of these "hogg troughs," paddled by three Indians, could easily outpace eight hard-rowing colonists.

Soon the Englishmen, with their steel-bitted axes and adzes, began to copy the Indian canoes. The dugout log boat perfectly matched the skills of untrained Europeans with the materials of the Chesapeake—trees so big that "three men with arms extended" could not reach around them. Occasionally the colonists widened their canoes into punts, first softening the sides by filling the boat with water and then dropping in red-hot rocks until the water boiled. This widened vessel gained some added stability, but only the most experienced waterman would care to fire his musket broadside from within a log canoe.

No More Big Trees

As the number of colonists grew, the forests correspondingly shrank. By the late eighteenth century, the huge trees of early days became increasingly scarce. Those that remained were often far from the waterside and troublesome to move. Legend has it that it was a slave named Aaron who solved the problem of the smaller trees. At his home on Lamb's Creek in York County, Virginia, he took two logs, hewed them square with an axe, and placed them side by side. With a piece of charcoal, he traced the lines of the boat on the top and sides. Then he separated the logs and shaped them each with an adz. From time to time, as the individual logs took shape, he reassembled the halves to gauge the evolving grace and symmetry of the craft by eye. No model or plan guided his work—it was strictly "winchum-squinchum."

First joining of the pines for a Chesapeake log sailing canoe.

The finished five-log canoe hull.

A Watertight Case

When Aaron had sculpted the timbers into 3-inch-thick half-shells, he had to fit them together with a perfectly watertight seam. Although time and a sharp blade could produce such a fit, Aaron may also have known the old shipwright's trick of "kerfing in." Starting at one end of the seam between the temporarily rope-bound timbers, he would have run his handsaw down the joint again and again. Each pass of the saw would take away an equal portion from each side of each tight place in the joint. When the saw teeth cut both sides for the whole length, the timbers were a perfect fit.

To join the halves, Aaron resorted to another ancient technique, the free tenon. Into the faces of the seams he cut a series of 1-inch-wide, 3-inch-long, 4-inch-deep mortices. Each mortice was matched to another in the opposite half. Into each mortice in one of the halves, he set an 8-inch-long oak tenon. He then forced the two halves together with twisted ropes and locked the tenons into place by driving locust pegs into holes bored through tenon and hull. Once in the water, the swelling timbers, restrained by the long grain of the oak tenons, forced the seams as tight as an oyster.

Later Aaron built a canoe from three logs, and then another from five logs. Soon, scores of these swift, graceful sailing craft were coursing the bay. Some were as long as 50 feet and built from as many as seven logs. Although the keel log could be made from a straight tree, the outer "wing" logs required appropriately curved trees, often found only after days of searching. The absence of internal ribbing made these undecked craft well suited to handling fish and oysters. Their incredible speed brought the catch to market far ahead of conventional sailboats.

One of these new sailboats, the *Buck Kelly*, became a favorite on the bay because of her unique history. The man who bought this 9-foot-wide, 50-foot-long, five-log "cunner" found her very fast, but too tricky in her handling to use as a workboat. In 1880 he hauled the craft to his boatyard, sawed it in half down its length, and added an extra 2-foot-wide log in the middle. Watermen stared and wondered at the now 11-foot-wide *Buck Kelly* when she passed. Thirty years later, this boat was lost in a fire, but dozens of her sister craft are preserved, still working the bay. Everyone loves a beautiful sailboat, but a boat with a story is irresistible.

A WOOD-AND-CANVAS KAYAK TO BUILD IN AN AFTERNOON

The only other thing they found here was a little skin boat or coracle on the sands. It was made of hide stretched over a wicker framework. It was a tiny boat, barely four feet long, and the paddle which still lay in it was in proportion.
– *C. S. Lewis,* The Voyage of the "Dawn Treader," *1952*

Rachell in the little kayak, made of scrap wood and an old dropcloth.

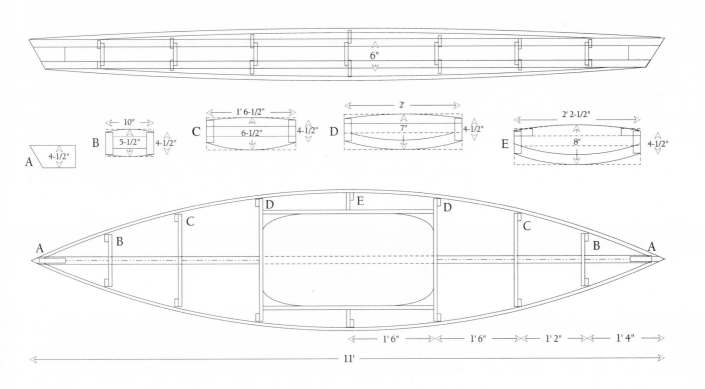

The kayak.

Nailing up the frames. The bottom curve was laid out by measuring the drop with straight lines, as if there were to be a V-shaped bottom, and then sketching in the curve by eye.

This kayak is not built to last, nor does it require any special skills, tools, or specially cut wood. You can build it today, this afternoon! It is light enough to carry in one hand—just a nailed-together wooden frame covered with canvas made waterproof with paint. This is a favorite project of the turn-of-the-century *Scientific American/Popular Mechanics* genre. It is, of course, based on an ancient concept. From the bark canoe to the skin-covered kayak to the seagoing Irish curach, the frame-and-skin craft is a quick way to get afloat. Short of inflating an ox skin, it is about the simplest boat you can make. The coracle is the English version of the frame-and-skin boat, woven like a basket, covered with cloth, and painted with tar. Rather than the ovoid shape of the coracle, this little boat follows the basic form of the Alaskan kayak. The frames are nailed in the English fashion into a structure that resembles the lines of latitude and longitude on a globe. First you make the frames (latitude), then you cover these frames with the longitudinal strakes from pole to pole, or stem to stern.

You can make this boat any size. Nine feet long is enough to support a passenger weighing about 90 pounds. An adult would need a 12 to 14 footer. This kayak can be made quite broad in the beam to make it more stable, but it is not a boat for whitewater. The canvas is easily torn, and you will sink. You can make the boat any size you want by drawing the outlines in chalk on the floor (the way French carpenters work) and then measuring the width at 18-inch intervals to find the dimensions for the cross frames. Remember that these frames will be covered with longitudinal strakes of about ¾-inch thickness. Therefore the frames must measure ¾ of an inch less *on all sides* than the final dimensions of the boat. This means that if the chalk diagram measures 18 inches from side to side at a given frame, the frame needs to be only 16½ inches wide at that point. The same holds true for measuring from top to bottom.

Measurements in hand, you next need to gather your wood. Rachell and I built her kayak from 1-by-3-inch pine and spruce pieces scavenged from the demolished scenery of a school play. We pulled the nails to reuse, but really, to keep the boat from rusting before it rots (it's a race), you should use bronze ring-shanked boat nails. These won't rust, and the rings on the shaft maintain such a good grip that you will not need to clinch them.

The side walls of each frame are flat and vertical and, for a 6-inch-high boat, measure 4½ inches each. Cut out as many as you need at one shot. The lower part of each frame is curved and so must be cut from a wider board—about a 1 by 4. Lay out the curve by first drawing straight lines from the ends to the center, as if the boat were to have a V-shaped bottom, and then draw a freehand curve connecting the three points. A minute or so with the hatchet shapes the convex face. You can delineate the inner curve accurately enough by holding a pencil in your knuckles so that it extends two inches in from the back of your hand as you run your knuckles down the previously curved face. Chop the inside curve and smooth as you see fit. You can also saw the curves if you are not comfortable with a hatchet and don't care to become so.

Nail each of the frames together, being careful to stagger the nails in the grain in triangular patterns to avoid splits. You may need to blunt the tips of the nails with your hammer to make them punch through the wood without splitting it. If you use common, smooth-shanked nails, you will need to drive them through and clinch them over to give them sufficient holding power. Nail the central frame together as a full rectangle just like the other frames. After the long strakes of the deck are on, you can cut out the top rail to open the cockpit.

When all of the frames are complete, begin joining the prime longitudinal pieces to their polar pieces, the stem and the stern. Make the stem and the stern from a length of 2-inch-thick stock, sawing it apart at a 60-degree angle. The boat curves more on the bottom, so choose the stiffer of the two best long strakes for the top side. This will help push the curve to the bottom. Measure out the locations for all of the frames, set them in place, square them up, and nail them in.

Nail the side strakes on in pairs to keep from distorting the frame with a permanent curve that will cause the kayak to go in circles. Do not nail

[left]

Nail the frames at their appointed intervals between the top and bottom strakes. The end pieces are cut from 2 by 6s at a 60-degree angle.

[right]

Rachell draws the side strakes together. Next they must be sawn off at the correct angle to nail flush to the stem and stern.

these side pieces flush with the edges of the frames. Rather, let them overhang by ¾ of an inch to match up with the ¾-inch strakes that will run the length of the top and bottom. If you have ripped your own strakes 2 inches wide, this will leave 1¼ inches to nail to the frames, which will be plenty.

With this overhang in mind, take two equally stiff strakes and nail their centers to the middle frame, one on each side. Throw a loop of rope with a slipknot around the ends of these long side strakes and begin pulling them together into the shape of the kayak. I don't know if this process is more exasperating with help or without it.

The bending will be much easier if the strakes are closer to ½ inch thick rather than ¾ inch. Near the shop is a mill that cuts "liners," the thin oak hoops that hold the lids of tobacco hogsheads. These are cut and bent from fresh green oak, and for years the mill has also sold strips to hunters for building boats just like this. Anyway, draw in the strakes and nail them as you go, moving outward from the center frame toward both ends and nailing both sides before re-tightening the ropes and nailing to the next pair of frames.

If working outward from the middle seems odd, you can use the more common of nailing the strakes to the stem and pulling them together at the stern. Either way, once they have been nailed to the side frames, pull the ends of the strakes hard against the sides of the stem and the stern. Now get out your ripsaw and eyeball the angle of cut that will make the strake fit flush against the end. Rip that cut, push it up flush, and nail it down. Proceed similarly on both sides of both ends, repeat with the second set of strakes, and you are ready to do the top and bottom.

The top and bottom take five strakes each. The center strake accounts for one, so just set four 1 by 2s evenly distributed on either side of the center line. The two outermost strakes on the top will form the sides of the cockpit opening, so be sure that they leave you ample room to get in. As with the side strakes, nail these to the center frame first and then move outward, nailing as you go. Where the ends of a top or bottom strake cross a side strake, eyeball the ripsaw right over the junction, saw through, and push the strake down flush with the top of the side strake. Nail the strake ends to the side strakes from the outside and inside of the boat and carry on until all are done.

[left]

Nail on more top and bottom strakes, sawing them off to fit within the side strakes.

[right]

Then push them down and nail them from outside and in.

Finish up the skeleton of the kayak by sawing out the cockpit opening. Notch the bottoms of the middle three frames to receive floor slats. It is awkward to reach into the cockpit to saw the notches at this point, but that's how it goes in the "fit-each-piece-to-the-one-that-went-in-before-it" school of boat building. Check the security of all the joints and remove any sharp corners with a plane to reduce the chances of their wearing through the canvas covering. Check for anything that might poke a hole and cause a leak.

The cheapest (yeah!) source for canvas is painters' dropcloths. These are often made from high-quality canvas in odd sizes, sewn together to make a suitably big piece. Do your best to find the piece with the fewest seams. Seams do not give much trouble if they are smooth, but buckles and bulges in the canvas are impossible to stretch out. Cover the bottom first by pulling the canvas up and around the stem and the stern and up into the sides of the cockpit. Tack it down into the top edge of the side strake at these four points with copper tacks. (You can use staples but they will rust pretty fast.) Working with a partner stationed on the opposite side, work your way from the middle of the boat down to the ends, pulling the canvas tight as you go. When you get to the ends, fold the extra back into a "hospital corner" and tack the flap down. Keep pulling out wrinkles and tacking all around until the frame is covered like a drum.

Now trim off the excess around the top and cover the top of the boat with the remaining canvas. Pull it tight and tack it around the edges. Cut the cockpit opening through the canvas, then pull the edges in around the rim and tack them tight. If you already have the quart of house paint you will need for waterproofing the canvas, paint the upper edge of the bottom canvas and stretch the top canvas over the still-wet paint to help seal the seam. The exterior house paint will do the job in one coat, but use as much as you think necessary.

With rot-resistant wood, bronze nails, copper tacks, and "reasonable care," you can make a kayak that will last many years. With scrap wood, box nails, and staples, you can make one that will last perhaps three years. Both will be great fun from the moment you hit the water.

ISHI

The starving man was cornered by snarling dogs. It was the morning of August 29, 1911, but he did not know that. He only knew that he was too weak to run from the dogs or the white-skinned men that were shouting strange words at him. Soon the men took him away to a room of smooth stone. The white-skins stared at him and called out to him through the iron bars. They brought him food, but it tasted too bad to eat. He wondered when they would kill him.

Cover the bottom with one continuous piece of canvas by pulling it up around the sides and tacking it tight. Stretch another piece over the top and paint with house paint. Wear a life jacket!

Ishi.

Two days later, a man carrying papers entered the room. The man sat beside him on the cot and began to say strange words as he pointed to things in the room. Finally the man shuffled his papers, pointed at the wooden cot, and said, "siwini." The dark-skinned man jumped—this white man knew the name of pine wood! He too pointed at the wood and said, "siwini," and for the next few moments the two of them banged on the wood of the cot, telling each other over and over, "siwini, siwini!"

The visitor was T. T. Waterman, an anthropologist from the University of California. The other man was Ishi, the only survivor of the Yahi Indians of Northern California, the last "wild" Indian in North America. Exhausted and alone, Ishi had walked out of the Stone Age and into a world of telephones, airplanes, and automobiles. With no other place to go, Ishi returned to San Francisco with Waterman. Eventually he took up residence at the city's Museum of Anthropology, where he was soon showing more than a thousand people a day his skill as a master woodcrafter.

Ishi showed his new friends how he made hunting bows from hickory, ash, yew, and mountain juniper. First he found the proper branch, split it into a rough billet, and set it aside to season slowly. Then, with obsidian knives, adzes, and scrapers, he brought the branch close to its final shape. For the final smoothing, he rubbed the bow with sandstone.

To recurve the ends of his bow, Ishi worked them over a heated stone until the wood became pliable. Carefully he bent the wood around his knee, holding it in place until it was cool and had set. Ishi treated his bow like a living thing, protecting it from heat and damp. Although he gradually began to acquire the possessions of white culture, Waterman recalled that "he loved his bow as he loved nothing else he owned."

Ishi also made his arrows in the ancient way of his people, always five at a time. He peeled the bark from hazel rods and then straightened them by rolling them on heated stones. After sandstoning the finished arrows, he polished them by rolling them on his thigh. Sometimes Ishi would add a foreshaft of heavier wood socketed into the mainshaft. After chipping a drill point from flint, he would hold it upright between his feet, and then roll the mainshaft between his palms to spin its end on the stationary point. When the socket in the end grain was about 1 inch deep, he would taper the other piece and glue the two together with pine resin.

Ishi's skill in shaping natural materials was typical of many Native Americans, who, like all traditional woodworkers, were expert at shaping wood by splitting. Eastern Indians split white oak and ash into strips for weaving baskets and fish traps. The Indians of the Pacific Northwest were adept at splitting planks from cedar logs to build their houses. They also understood how split wood could be bent to make such items as snowshoes, boxes, lacrosse sticks, and skin-covered kayaks.

Perhaps the finest expression of these skills was the birch-bark canoe, in which spruce roots were used to lash the spruce thwarts and gunwales

[opposite]

Ishi making a bow with a hatchet.

Lashing the prongs of a fishing spear.

to the white cedar ribs and bottom. The canoe builder used an ingenious method to bend the prow piece of the canoe. He repeatedly split a cedar billet halfway down its length until he had divided the wood into dozens of thin leaves like the pages of a book. It could be readily bent, the leaves sliding easily past one another, yet retained its strength like laminated wood. A 14-foot bark canoe weighed only 50 pounds—easily carried by one man.

The Crooked Knife

From the earliest days of contact, the Europeans marveled at the skill of Native American woodcarvers. From Seminole dugouts to the grotesque masks carved from living trees by the Iroquois, the Indians proved themselves to be superb sculptors. John Lawson, the British explorer, wrote in 1709, "I have known an Indian stock Guns better than most of our Joiners, although he never saw one stock'd before: . . . and besides, his Working-Tool was only a sorry Knife." Lawson also noticed that "When they cut with a Knife, the Edge is towards them, wheras we always cut and whittle from us."

The tool he was describing may have been the crooked knife. John Franklin, another British explorer, was impressed with the Indians' virtuosity with this tool. In 1824 he wrote: "The crooked knife, generally made of an old file, bent and tempered by heat, serves an Indian . . . for plane, chisel and auger. With it the snow-shoe and canoe timbers are fashioned, the deals of their sledges reduced to the requisite thinness and polish, and their wooden bowls and spoons hollowed out."

The crooked knife may have begun as a beaver tooth set in a bone handle. But, just as the horse profoundly affected the culture of the Plains Indians, the abundant steel blades brought over by the Europeans allowed Indian artistic prowess to explode. We know this mainly from the work of the Northwest Indians, whose shallow designs on house posts evolved into high-relief totem poles with the aid of the new tools. Canoes, bowls, and ceremonial masks took on a fantastic aspect. Sadly, the carving of the eastern woodland Indians, which may have been as sophisticated as that of the Northwest Indians, is all gone. Most of it was destroyed well before the new American civilization was mature enough to appreciate it.

During the five years that Ishi lived after his introduction to modern America, he offered a priceless window into his vanished world. Since his death, experimental archaeologists have explored the technology of the Stone Age by attempting to make and use stone tools. They have learned to chip and polish the cutting edges, to properly affix the handles, and then to use the tools on wood. But whereas their work shows only what was possible with stone tools, Ishi shared first-hand his mastery of the craftsmanship of the first Americans.

A modern crooked knife thinning the end of a toboggan.

This toboggan is designed to ride in the tracks of your snowshoes. Because the bent oak runners are lashed to the split-sapling cross pieces, the toboggan can flex with irregularities in the trail.

[opposite]

After first bending the runners individually and lashing them together with copper wire, immerse the whole bent end in boiling water and rebend around a log to help even them out.

TOBOGGAN

I saw this toboggan in a book by one of my favorite childhood authors, William Ben Hunt. The picture showed a man standing beside a 55-gallon drum suspended over a fire, with the end of a toboggan boiling away. The man displayed all the nonchalance of someone fixing a cup of tea. For a kid from my background, a 55-gallon drum was about as exotic as a cape buffalo. One day, though, I too would boil a toboggan.

Thirty years later, a heavy snow promised to linger for a few days. We had no time to waste. We found the longest split-oak clapboards in town. Northern toboggans are usually of cedar or ash, but oak will do in a pinch. Another image from Hunt's book was that of a crooked knife, held in confident hands, thinning down the end of the board before bending it. The knife catches easily in the grain of the oak, so most of the work has to proceed across the grain as you gradually thin the ½-inch-thick oak down to a scant ⅜ of an inch.

Here's an excellent way to sand the bottom.

Toboggans gain strength from their flexibility. Lashing the runners to the crosspieces with sinews or heavy copper wire will hold far longer than nails or screws in such thin material. Make these crosspieces from split hickory sticks. Notch each stick on the flat side near the ends to hold the tow rope, which runs the full length of the toboggan. Drill holes through the runners for the copper wire and, on the underside that rides on the snow, join the two holes with a groove just deep enough to house the wire. Slip the loop of wire through the holes and around the cross stick and twist the end tight with a pair of pliers.

As in my favorite picture, the end of the toboggan needs to be boiled for an hour or more to soften it up for bending. The process is straightforward enough: you boil the end and then bend it around a log and hold it until it sets up—at least a full day. I have found it safer to bend the two slats separately and then join them together, having seen enough wood crack upon bending to be wary of putting this step last in the construction process. If you crack a piece that is already joined to another, all the previous work must be undone.

The tow rope slips under the notches cut for them in the cross bars, and a separate rope goes up to hold back the curved end. The bottom will benefit from sanding. If you have steep dunes nearby, the kids will gladly do this last part for you.

6 Musical Instruments

Though you may fret me, yet you
cannot play upon me.

– William Shakespeare, *Hamlet*, 1601

[overleaf]

The mountain dulcimer in its most familiar form.

Appalachian Dulcimer

There is something daunting to the novice about making stringed instruments. They look hard to do, but you *can* make a dulcimer, particularly if you can borrow one to copy. You will do well to copy one that you like, but if you prefer, you can follow the dimensions I give here and end up with another one like the one I borrowed. The process I describe should adapt to any design. If you have a good guitar shop nearby, you can usually arrange to get hold of a dulcimer for long enough to copy it, and you can buy strings, fretwire, and even pegs. This leaves you with eight or fewer pieces of wood to shape and glue together into a box that sings.

Any good instrument begins with good wood that has been given enough time to dry. You may even cut a tree with the instrument in mind. Split pieces for the sides, head, and fretboard from a green walnut log, thin them down, and put them away. Salvage an old poplar board from a hog pen to use for the face and back. Clean it up and bring it inside to dry. It all starts with good wood, you add the drying, and then you shape all the parts and glue them together.

Start the head (called the scroll if you use the traditional snailshell carving) by sawing its outline from a 1¼-inch-thick piece of walnut (or maple, or whatever hardwood you wish). The scroll is the traditional finial for a violin, but as a decoration, it could just as well be the carved head of Elvis. The peg hollow is the place in the center of the head where the strings wind around the tuning pegs. Lay out the hollow with a double-toothed morticing gauge, making sure to leave the side walls at least 5⁄16 inch thick to give the pegs sufficient grip. You can rough out the peg hollow quickly by boring in at the scroll end with a 5⁄8 inch auger, sawing down along the grain, and then finishing up with a chisel.

Whether you like the looks of your head or not, without well-set tuning pegs your instrument will not be playable. The pegs are simply levers that allow you to increase or decrease the tension of the strings and wedges that hold the adjustment once it's made. Achieving the friction fit of the gently tapered pegs requires considerable patience and care. It is possible to buy or make matched peg shavers and reamers that make the job quick and easy, but I took the advice of a violin maker and bought viola pegs at an instrument shop and fitted them by trial and error. Drive a peg in hard and turn it so that it leaves shiny places on the interior walls of the peg hole, then carefully remove the shiny spots with a rat-tail file. There is a point of no return at which the hole becomes too big for the peg to fit tightly. For this reason, it's a good idea to finish the head and make sure its pegs are in working trim before you join it to the other parts.

The head and the tailpiece connect the sides like the stem and stern of a boat. The sides meet these pieces at an angle, which can be formed with a saw kerf or an open shoulder. The saw kerf will glue up without clamping, but it makes later repairs tougher.

Start the scroll by sawing it to the rough shape and sawing the slots to hold the sides. Rough in the peg hollow by boring a hole at the end, sawing down the sides, and chiseling out the wood in between.

Bending

On most familiar dulcimers, the sides are serpentine—not just for looks, but for strength as well. The curved sides resist pressure in the same way that a curved beaverdam does. Straight-grained wood shaved down to ⅟16-inch thickness will bend with little trouble. You can easily ripsaw down the edge of 1½-inch-thick wood for 3 feet to make this thin stock. Take good care as you plane down to the final smoothness and thickness. Any grabbing and tearing of the grain will weaken the wood at that point and cause it to snap or bend unevenly. Using a scraper and constantly checking for thick spots (you can't do much about thin spots) is a safe way to work. Interesting wood, like interesting people, can be challenging to work with.

Successful bending of the sides, then, starts with the right wood carefully brought to an even thinness. Bending against a hot pipe exploits the plastic nature of wood by softening the lignin and cellulose so that they bend easily and take a permanent set when the wood cools. Some workers use more water in this process than others, but the object is not to steam or soak the wood into limpness (although some work that way). Dampen the wood just enough to keep the surface that comes in contact with the hot iron from scorching.

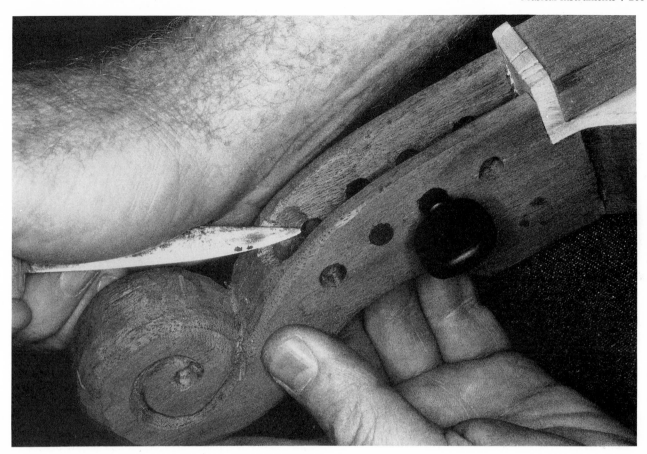

Start bending a curve by heating the opposite (convex) face of the bend. Keep the wood moving over the surface of the pipe. When it gets good and hot, flip it over and, still constantly moving the wood, push down to bend it. You will feel the wood give once it is hot enough. If you bend wood around a hot stovepipe, you will know not to push too hard or you will knock the pipe loose from the woodstove and cause a fire.

Bend the sides until they match the traced paper pattern of the dulcimer you are copying. As you gain experience, you will find places where you want to overbend or underbend to build tension into the instrument, but for now, just try to get it on the line. Hold each curve until it is cool and it will stay put with very little springback.

Fit the pegs in holes gently tapered with a rat-tail file. The boxwood nut fits between the scroll and the fretboard.

Soundboard and Back

Making the soundboard and the back is going to put you through some heavy ripsawing. You can do it—it just takes a little time. I used an old, green-hearted tulip poplar board from a hog pen and sawed it into two ⅛-inch-thick sheets, 7 inches wide, ready for planing. The sawing takes about thirty minutes for each cut, which gives you ample time to contemplate your recent misdeeds. You could make the job easier by cutting in around the edges with a circular saw and just finishing up the middle with

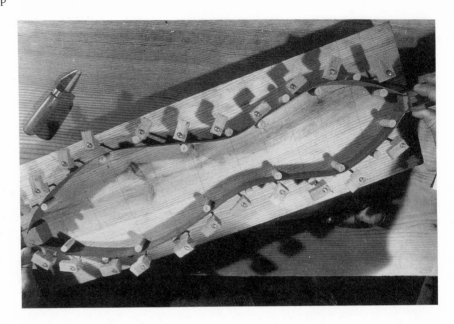

Bend the sides by holding them against a hot stovepipe. A gluing frame holds the sides as they are glued into the scroll and tailpiece. This frame will serve through the whole assembly process.

[opposite]
Carefully cut the soundholes through the thin top by boring three holes in a cloverleaf pattern and finishing with a knife. The heart is just one of the most common soundhole patterns; the countless variations are distinctive as makers' marks.

the handsaw. You could also rip wood 3½ inches thick and glue the two halves together along the center edge into a "book match." This is how fine instruments are made to ensure symmetrical density.

Another tactic is to find wood that is already cut pretty thin. I have often heard of instruments made from dynamite cases. The dynamite doesn't impart any special tone, but the nitroglycerine absorbed by the wood can give you a terrific headache. The point with the dynamite cases is that the wood is already thin enough that it can be brought the rest of the way down with a plane. These days you can often find wooden crating sawn from tropical trees, some of which must be giant poison ivy trees, because the sawdust has the same irritating effect on your skin. In any case, stop planing the stuff when it gets below ⅛ inch thick—1⁄16 inch is too thin.

By now you know what a pain it is to get thin, flat wood and how bad you would feel if you were to accidentally crack the back or soundboard while sawing it to shape. You will find that it's safer to cut the outline by keeping the wood flat against a flat board as you slice in with a sharp, thin-bladed knife in several deepening passes. Be sure to cut the outline oversized by ⅛ inch all around. You can either trim it up flush or leave a slight overhang after you have glued it to the sides.

Just as the archetypal dulcimer has double-curved sides (like the traditional male two-handed sign for a woman's figure), it typically has four heart-shaped soundholes in the face. Variations in the soundhole design and placement are the distinctive signatures of individual makers. You can make the conventional heart quickly by boring three holes in a triangle and then finishing the shape with a knife. You can also ruin a lot of work by accidentally splitting the soundboard with the screwpoint of the auger. Either predrill clearance for the screwpoint or use a center bit that has a center pike rather than a leadscrew. If you are going to hollow out the

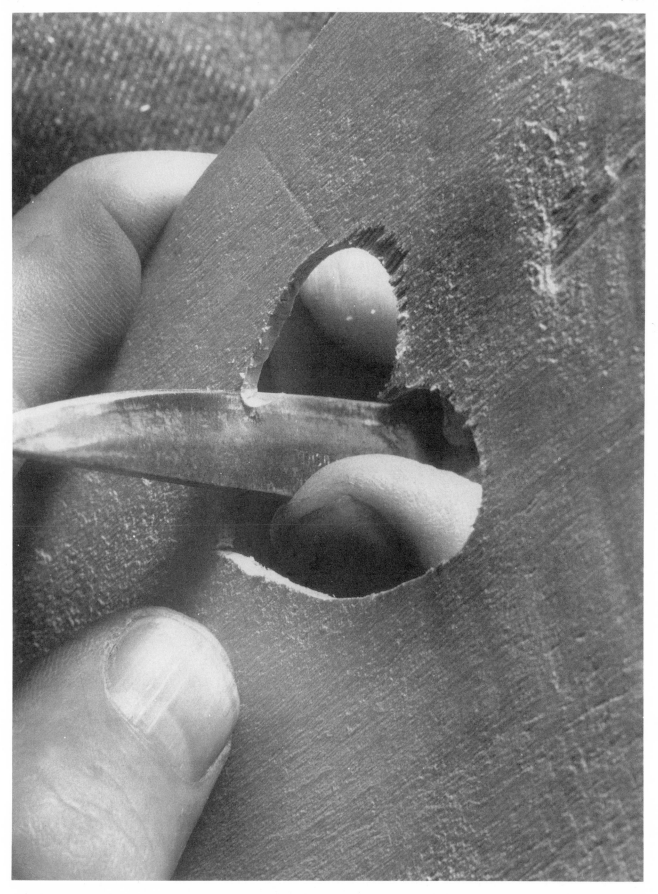

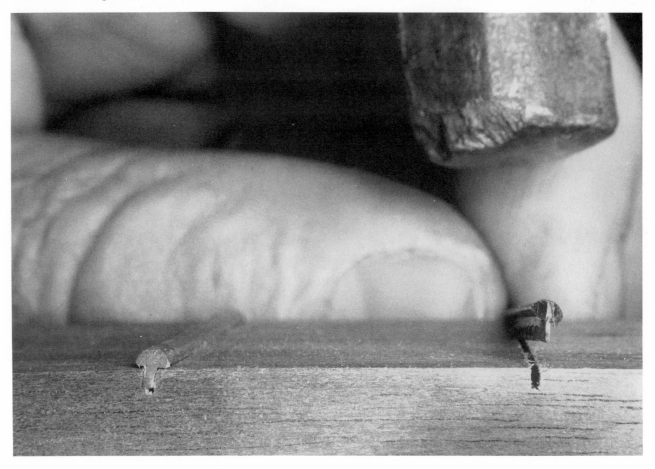

Fretwire is T-shaped to fit in slots sawn across the fretboards. You can buy it from an instrument repair shop.

underside of the fretboard (which comes next), you should also cut the long openings into the top beneath where the fretboard will be glued by this same method of boring first and slicing out.

Fretboard

Although you cut hearts in the soundboard, the real heart of the instrument is the fretboard. It must have both strength and precision. When you press a string down onto a fret, the free-vibrating length must not buzz against the next fret down. The most precisely made fretboard can become unplayable if it warps. Use all the precautions available against warping: straight, even grain; dry wood; and second seasoning. Second seasoning means shaping the wood very close to its final dimensions and then setting it aside to dry some more before you make that final pass with the jointer plane.

As I mentioned earlier, many dulcimer makers hollow the underside of the fretboard. This lightens the fretboard while allowing it to retain much of its stiffness. Although you will find it a simple task to hollow the back, do it first and let the fretboard sit for a few days before the final planing.

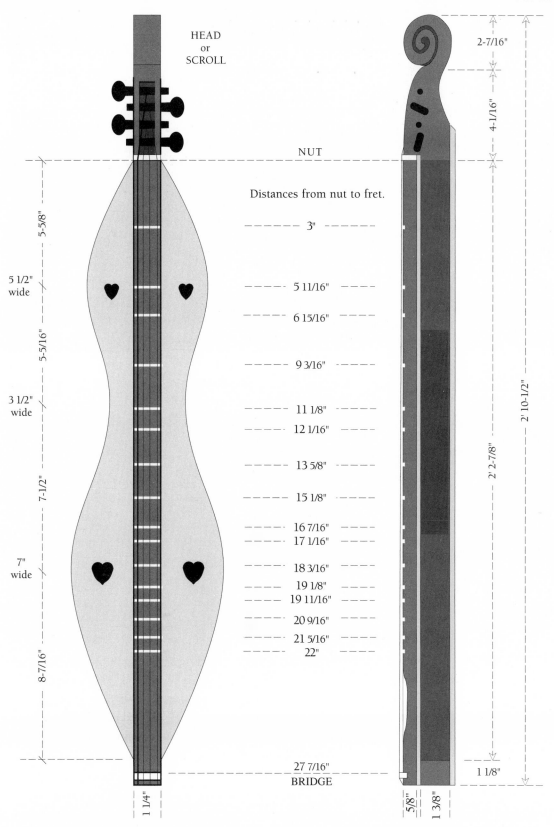

HEAD
or
SCROLL

2-7/16"

4-1/16"

NUT

Distances from nut to fret.

3"

5 11/16"

6 15/16"

9 3/16"

11 1/8"

12 1/16"

13 5/8"

15 1/8"

16 7/16"

17 1/16"

18 3/16"

19 1/8"

19 11/16"

20 9/16"

21 5/16"

22"

27 7/16"

BRIDGE

2' 2-7/8"

2' 10-1/2"

1 1/8"

5-5/8"

5 1/2"
wide

5-5/16"

3 1/2"
wide

7-1/2"

7"
wide

8-7/16"

1 1/4"

5/8"

1 3/8"

The Appalachian dulcimer.

After gluing the fretboard to the soundboard, glue the top to the sides, tailpiece, and scroll, first clamping them together in the gluing frame.

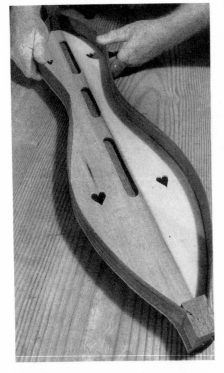

Ready for the bottom. You can see the hollow in the underside of the fretboard through the elongated holes in the top. This is supposed to give the dulcimer a better tone, but I take this on faith because I can't hear it.

The face of the fretboard receives the frets and the strum hollow. The strum hollow is a simple cutaway place near the tail end of the fretboard that gives clearance for picking and strumming when you play. The frets need to be laid out in the precise spacing given in the table or copied from your model. The frets themselves can be made either with T-shaped fretwire (which you buy from an instrument repair shop) driven into a fine saw kerf or with wire staples driven into predrilled holes. If you buy fretwire, buy enough to practice with.

The saw kerf must be well matched to the size of the wire and the hardness of the wood. The wire needs to be a tight fit, but not so tight that it exerts a wedging action on the fretboard and bows it back when all the wires have been driven in. Softer wood will give more and can take fretwire in a narrower kerf than a hardwood like ebony. Make sure you have the right combination before you proceed. Wet the kerf with a single drop of water and tap the fretwire in at one end with a smooth-faced hammer. Continue tapping down the fretwire until it is seated across the whole face of the board and snip off the end. When all frets are in place, bevel their ends with a file. As a final assurance that the frets are all level, dress them with a large, flat, smooth file, sliding it up and down the frets until they are all brightened by its passage. This will leave sharp corners that you will need to round with files or abrasives.

The bridge and the nut hold the strings above the fretboard. They need to be made of very hard stuff to keep the wire from biting in. They also offer a chance to make some color contrast among the woods. Boxwood or bone each look sharp inset against a walnut fretboard. The bridge at the foot of the instrument can be either free-moving or inset. Although insetting the bridge will keep it from slipping, don't glue it into place. This will enable you to make height and depth adjustments should you need them. The nut fits between the fretboard and the head in the same way.

Assembly

To help you assemble this curvy box, you will need to make a combined bending jig and gluing frame, or mold. This is simply a flat board fitted with pegs to hold the dulcimer sides and screw-down clamps (a bunch of woodscrews and wooden blocks) to hold the dulcimer under pressure as the glue dries. Start making the mold by tracing the outline of the dulcimer on the board, then locate the centers for eleven pegs on each side. Make sure that a peg resides within the nadir of each concavity, matching the peg locations on both sides. Bore all the holes for the pegs to the same depth, or go all the way through. These pegs must be removable, and they

Set the bottom down in the gluing frame and then glue the top assembly down on it.

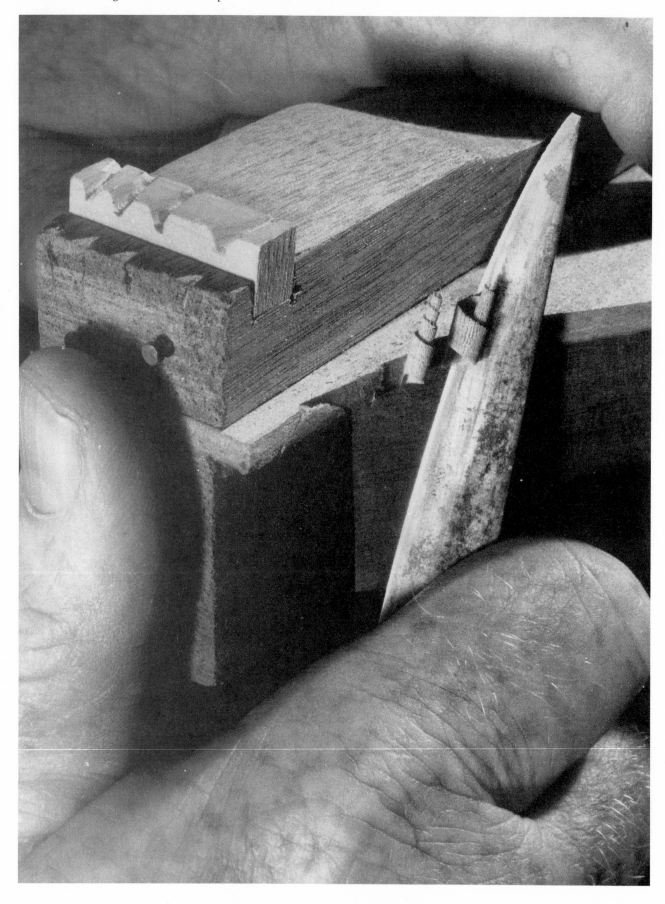

must protrude ⅛ inch less than the height of the sides. Situate eleven wood screws evenly up and down each side, far enough back from the line to let the turnbutton swing clear (about ⅜ inch).

When all the parts are ready to go together, use good hide glue and join the parts in the following sequence:

- Glue the bent sides to the head and tailpiece in the mold.
- On a flat table, glue the fretboard to the soundboard.
- When these two subassemblies are dry, glue them together in the mold by running a thin bead of glue around the top of the sides, head and tailpiece, setting the top and fretboard in place, and clamping it down with the turnbuttons and woodscrews.
- When the top has set overnight, remove it from the mold, pull out the inner set of pegs, and drop in the back. Affix your label or sign your name on the inside of the bottom where you can see it through one of the sound holes in the top. (So that's how they do it!) Run a bead of glue around the underedge of the assembled top and sides and set it down on the bottom. Turn down the screws and let it dry again overnight.

When you remove the finished dulcimer from the mold, trim the edges with your knife, either flush with the sides or with a slight overhang. Carefully sand the instrument all over and finish it with varnish. You can either buy dulcimer strings or use banjo second strings and one banjo fourth string for the bass. Drive a stout pair of nails or screws into the tailpiece to anchor the strings and wind the other end onto the pegs. There are many alternate ways of tuning a dulcimer, but I have to leave you to the wisdom of others at this point. I know how to put the music into the wood, but I leave it to my betters to get it back out.

WALKING-STICK FLUTE

Guil.: *I know no touch of it, my lord.*
Ham.: *It is as easy as lying. Govern these ventages with your fingers and thumb, give it breath with your mouth, and it will discourse most eloquent music. Look you, these are the stops.*
– William Shakespeare, Hamlet, *1601*

Flutes and recorders are fun to make and to play. You can work in a small space, you don't need a lot of wood or too many special tools to get started, and the opportunities for improvement are abundant. Best of all, not everybody's doing it. Making flutes and recorders basically just requires some augers and chisels. You will also need a lathe with a hollow center at one end, but you can make this yourself. The simple proce-

[opposite]

Trim the top to match the sides, either flush or with a slight overhang. The boxwood bridge is set into a notch in the end of the fretboard. The nails in the end grain anchor the loops of the strings.

The walking-stick flute and the boxwood recorder.

dure consists of boring an initial small hole through the length of a stick, reboring the hole to a stepped taper, reaming the taper smooth, then finishing up with the fingerholes. A recorder is harder to make than a flute, so we will begin with a fife.

Bamboo Fife

We start with the bamboo fife because the borehole is already there. The outside is finished as well, so you don't need a lathe. All you need to do is cut a piece to the required length, break through a node if need be, cut the mouth hole (or embouchure, as it is properly called), cut the fingerholes, and learn how to play.

Well, that was quick. I hope you remembered from making the Balinese whirligig how to put a hole through bamboo without splitting it. You may just want to use a node as the stop; otherwise, cut a cork to sit just an embouchure's diameter away from the embouchure. You will occasionally find bamboo that has turned dusty black. This polishes to a brilliant ebony. Polish with a cloth, but no more than that. The surface of bamboo is very delicate and shows scratches quite plainly.

Wooden Flute

You need good wood to make flutes and recorders. Michala Petri, the Danish virtuoso, plays recorders made from grenadilla, or African blackwood, a rare relative of rosewood. "It makes the tones that project the best in the big concert halls." She has many recorders, all made to the same specifications, "but still they turn out very different, because wood is a living material." The rest of us will consider ourselves most fortunate to acquire boxwood or pear wood to make recorders from. You may have to poke about to find one of these rarer woods, but in the meantime, hard maple or cherry will do well and are generally available. If you cut fresh wood, put it aside for as long as you can to allow it to season.

If you doubt your ability to tell when the wood is dry, weigh it every few weeks, recording the weight each time. When the wood stops losing weight, it has reached equilibrium with the moisture in its environment. Small pieces will dry faster than fatter ones. You may wish to work the wood down into billets measuring about 1½ inches in diameter and an inch or so longer than the desired final length of the instrument. The wood will also dry faster if you bore out a pilot hole down the length, but this creates a potential problem with warping, which would require you to rebore the hole—but it's worth a try. Cow dung is apparently just as good as wax for sealing the end grain to prevent cracking, but I would not use it for making wind instruments.

My favorite instrument, the bamboo fife. All you need is the grass and a knife.

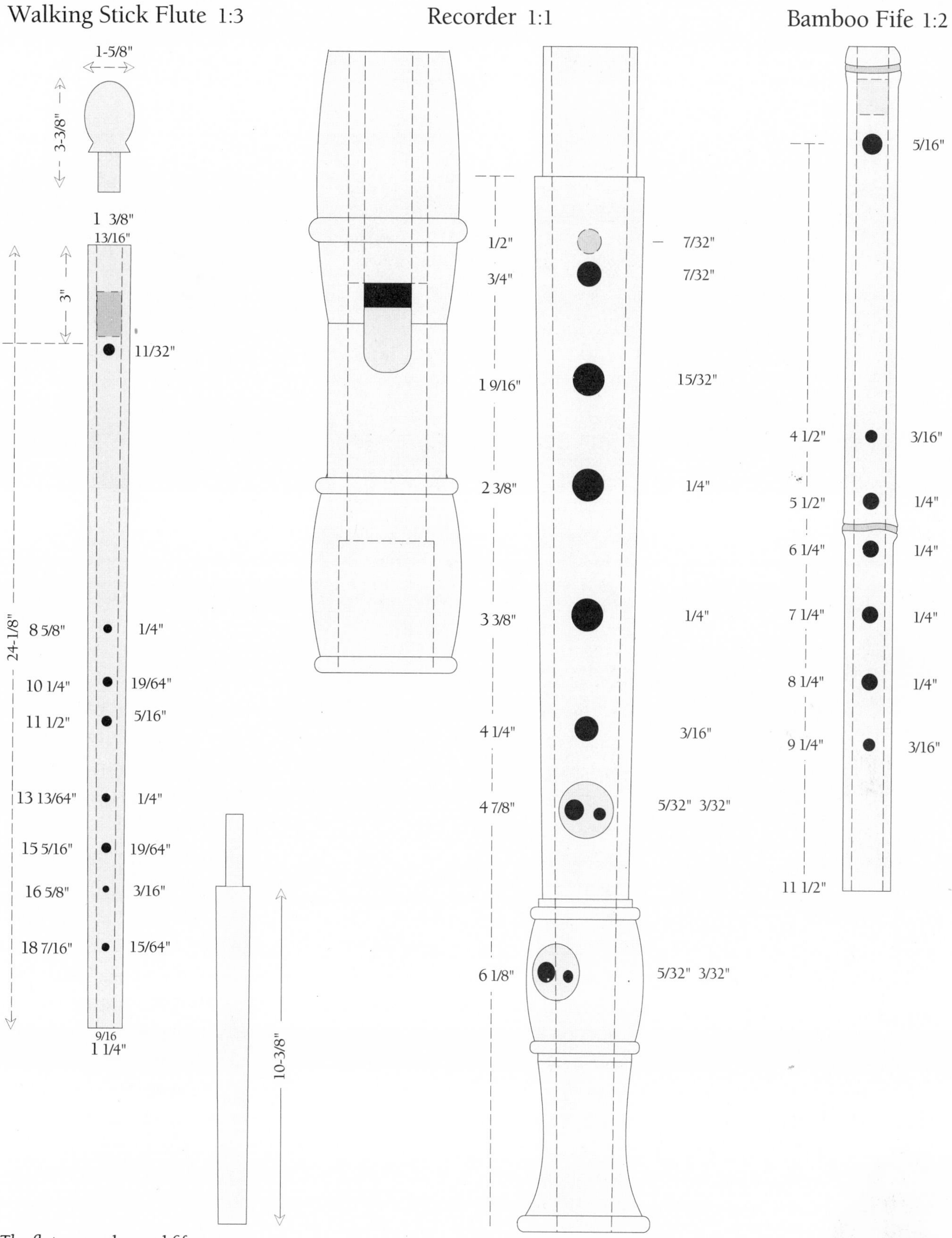

Walking Stick Flute 1:3

1-5/8"

3-3/8"

1 3/8"
13/16"

3"

11/32"

24-1/8"

8 5/8"   1/4"

10 1/4"   19/64"

11 1/2"   5/16"

13 13/64"   1/4"

15 5/16"   19/64"

16 5/8"   3/16"

18 7/16"   15/264"

9/16
1 1/4"

10-3/8"

Recorder 1:1

1/2"   7/32"

3/4"   7/32"

1 9/16"   15/32"

2 3/8"   1/4"

3 3/8"   1/4"

4 1/4"   3/16"

4 7/8"   5/32" 3/32"

6 1/8"   5/32" 3/32"

Bamboo Fife 1:2

5/16"

4 1/2"   3/16"

5 1/2"   1/4"

6 1/4"   1/4"

7 1/4"   1/4"

8 1/4"   1/4"

9 1/4"   3/16"

11 1/2"

The flute, recorder, and fife.

Bore the inside of the flute (or other instrument) on the lathe using a hollow center made from a brass plumbing tee. The auger in the picture is a lipped "nose auger." Although these cut straightest, an electrician's twisty bit or even a spade bit will do as well.

A Hollow Center

Before you can bore the length of the flute or recorder on the lathe, you must make a special tool called a hollow center. A hollow center holds one end of the spinning wood and allows you to pass an auger through it into the end grain. I suppose you can buy this tool, but most people make one from a brass plumbing tee. This is a T-shaped joint for connecting three pieces of pipe. Turn a hickory-hard shaft to fit tightly through the long top of the tee. Force this shaft through the tee and fit it back into the lathe. Hold a file against one end of the spinning tee and turn it down to a sharp edge all around. Keep the lathe speed way down and stand off to one side—the off-center brass tee can be thrown from the lathe with killing speed. With an added length of pipe, this hollow center can fit in the tool rest mount of an iron lathe. On a wooden lathe, you can easily make an extra wooden tail stock to hold it.

Mandrels and Turning

Before the flute blank can go in the lathe, you need to make a place in its end for the hollow center to fit. A twist auger will do this very well. Turn it in by hand just enough for the lips to make a track. Rub a little beeswax in the track before you mount the stock. To keep any off-centeredness from

wasting energy as you bore, turn the outside to a cylinder of roughly the final size.

You can bore with almost any auger that doesn't have a lead screw. Electricians' installer bits are long enough and are easily available. (You can also buy or make the proper kind of lipped cylinder auger, but the installer bit will get you started.) Begin by boring down the whole length with a ⅜-inch drill, then follow with a ½-inch spade bit. The spade bit will stay centered by the first pilot hole. Be sure to pull the drill back and clear out the dust every few seconds or it will become hopelessly jammed.

Whatever drill you use, don't bore so far down that you hit the center on the far end. To complete the bore, you need to reverse the piece in the lathe, prepare the unbored end to fit in the hollow center, and make a little mandrel to help you center the previously bored end in the lathe. The mandrel is quick to make. Set a good piece of hardwood in the lathe, turn it true, and then turn it down until it fits snugly within the bore of the flute. Push the mandrel into the end of the bored-out piece, return the whole affair to the lathe, and bore that last little bit.

This flute has a tapered bore, so now you need to enlarge the hole in two stages. First, rebore down two-thirds of the length with a ⅝-inch bit, then rebore one-third of the length again with a ¾-inch bit. These stepped holes will make a workable flute, but you can readily make a reamer to smooth the bore.

When one end has been bored to the final size, remove the flute from the lathe and insert a mandrel turned to fit snugly in the bore. Return the flute to the lathe with the ends reversed and bore into the other end until the holes meet.

Reamers

Professional steel reamers are plenty expensive, but you can make a perfectly good one from hickory and a hacksaw blade. Choose a piece of hickory or other hardwood and turn it down to just under the size and taper of the final bore that you want. Now take a fine backsaw and cut a ¼-inch deep slot down the length of the shaft. This slot will hold the cutting blade, which you can shear off from a hacksaw or bandsaw blade, cutting it lengthwise with tinsnips. Drive this blade into the slot and then sharpen it by sliding a file down its length. Leave less than ¹⁄₁₆ inch of the blade protruding from the diameter of the hickory shaft. Try the scraper out by inserting it into the stepped hole and turning it clockwise. The hole will need to be cleared of scrapings frequently. You may want to cut a space for the scrapings to gather on the leading edge of the blade, but try it out before you cut too much. The more you cut away, the weaker the reamer gets, and the more tenuous its grip on the blade.

Fingerholes and Finish

Once the hole has been bored and reamed, you can return the flute to the lathe and turn the outside to its final shape. The thickness of the cylinder walls affects the depth of the fingerholes, which in turn affects the pitch of the instrument. To some degree the pitch can be corrected by changing the placement of the cork stopper. My earlier guideline of an offset equal to the diameter of the embouchure is just for starters. If you do not have a flute to copy, you can use the measurements for the placement and diameters of the fingerholes that I have listed here. A good way to transfer measurements from one flute to another is by using a long strip of paper. Hold the strip on the flute you want to copy and run your finger down its length to leave impressions of the fingerholes on the paper.

BOXWOOD RECORDER

If you were to mention a flute to eighteenth-century Europeans, they would think of what we recognize today as a recorder. The recorder lost popularity at the end of the eighteenth century and essentially disappeared until its twentieth-century revival. A recorder is a bit more difficult to make than a transverse flute, but it is much easier to play. All you have to do is blow in one end and you get a sound.

A recorder is easier to finger, too. It has only eight holes, and you probably have ten fingers. Each finger belongs to only one hole and never has to move. You will see the reason for the exterior shape as you handle the instrument. The bulbous thickening of the socket end reinforces it

Bring the bore to the final taper with a hickory (or other very hard wood) reamer with a hacksaw blade cutter.

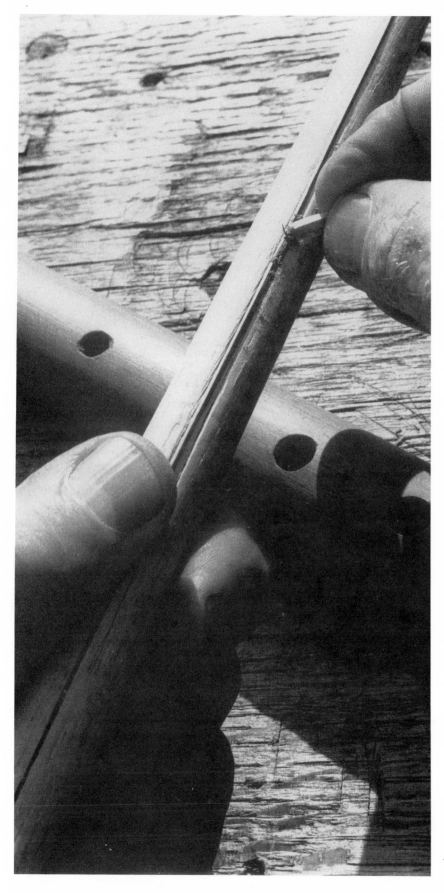

The blade will need to be cleared frequently of scrapings, but it works surprisingly fast.

The steps in making the top piece of the recorder. Starting on the left, the rough blank is bored through. Next the exterior is turned on the lathe with the aid of mandrels inserted into the end. Then the windway and window are cut and the red cedar fipple inserted. Finally, the mouthpiece is cut away. This finished piece is boxwood; the others are pear.

against splitting. The thickening at the mouthpiece adds strength. The recorder requires a 6-inch section for the top piece and a 10-inch section for the lower piece. I make the lower section of a single piece of wood but, like many makers, retain the bulbosity of those that are made with a lower joint.

Top Piece

Unlike the flute, the top of the recorder can be made by first boring the hole through the length of the rough billet with a regular brace and bit. You then place it in the lathe and turn the exterior concentric to that axis. Bore the larger socket hole first, then center the auger for the smaller fipple hole within it and continue to bore the rest of the way through. The socket of the top piece of the recorder must be made larger than the rest of the bore to prevent a sudden change in the diameter of the interior bore at the joint. A well-sharpened ¾-inch spade or spiral bit and considerable pressure will do the trick. The end grain of boxwood is about as hard as wood gets. If the cutting edge of your auger is dubbed over, you will get nowhere.

Bore the socket ⅞ inch deep, but include in this depth the cut made by the scoring lips on the perimeter of your spiral auger, should you use one. The wood scored by these lips will soon break out as the inner hole is bored. Change to the ⅝-inch bit for this inner or fipple bore. The smaller bit will find the center left by the larger one. Here you see another good reason to bore first, turn second. The thicker billet is much less likely to be split by the passage of the auger than would a cylinder already turned down to its final diameter.

A regular spiral auger will bore the top piece if it is sharp enough. Bore the larger hole for the socket to attach the foot first, then bore the smaller hole for the fipple within it to pass the rest of the way through.

Begin the mouth by drilling two small holes that can be enlarged with chisels. The rope around the recorder passes through a hole in the bench top down in a loop by the floor where it can be held with foot pressure.

As you did with the flute, turn mandrels to fit into the ends of the recorder so that it can fit in the lathe. Check that the fit of the mandrel is not so snug that you will risk cracking open the top piece, which is going to become thinner-walled as the work progresses.

In turning boxwood, you cannot proceed with the same verve as you might with softer stuff. You can shape the boxwood with gouges, but when you get down to the closer cuts, you will do better by scraping. You can make scrapers from old files that have been sharpened to an abrupt angle on the edge. With scrapers, you need to set the tool rest close to the work and hold the handle end high so that the point of contact is about level with the axis of rotation. Joseph Moxon aptly described the work of boxwood turners in his 1678 *Mechanick Exercises*: "Holding the basil'd Edge of the Knife close against the Work while it comes about: For then its sharp Edge scrapes or shaves off the little roughness the grosser *Tools* left upon the Work."

Cutting the Mouth

Making the mouth opening is the most critical step, for once this cut is made, the voice of the instrument is established. I have made too many recorders with a mouth that was too open, giving them a breathy voice. The mouth begins as a row of ⅛-inch-diameter holes drilled at the shoulder of the turned ring. A dismounted coping saw blade should fit into one of the holes, allowing you to join them with a cut wide enough that a file can then be inserted to bring the mouth to a proper rectangle.

The fragile, turned cylinder must be held firmly during these operations, but you don't want to crush it in the vise, either. The best way of holding it is to use a long loop of sash cord set through a hole in the bench top. Put the recorder through the loop on top of the bench and your foot through the loop that hangs beneath the bench. The same arrangement will hold the work as you carefully chisel the mouth to its final shape.

Carefully chisel the ramp down to the sharp windcutter.

Windway

The windway is the slot chiseled into the wall of the fipple bore that channels the air into collision with a sharp lip. Set the top piece on a peg that is in turn set into the top of the bench and, with a ⅜-inch chisel, start down at the mouth and work your way back, paring out a ⅛-inch-deep slot.

The fipple will block the rest of the mouth-end bore, making the windway the only place for air to pass through. The fipple will also get pretty wet as you play. If the fipple wood swells more with moisture than the outer wood, the outside will split. Use red cedar, which will expand less than other wood due to the resins that render it less permeable.

Turn the fipple to a snug fit within the bore. Try the fit and then chisel a ⅜-inch-wide flat face down one side, corresponding to the flat chiseled within the bore. Now split out and pare smooth a sliver of cedar, ⅜ inch wide and a fat ¹⁄₁₆ inch thick, that you can glue to the flat on the fipple to make the windway narrow down to a scant ¹⁄₁₆ inch at the mouth end.

The lip of the recorder is the sharp edge that forces the air stream into oscillation. Insert a turned blank of wood into the bore to support the lip as you chisel it. The lip needs to be flat on the inside as well, so you must reach in from the socket end to shape it. Try to keep the mouth from growing wider. The sharp edge of the lip should sit just below the the middle of the windway. Once you have finished the sharpening, you can try out the tone. There ought to be a special name for the first note to come from a block of wood.

When you are happy with fipple and its relationship to the mouth (you may need to move it in and out to find the best tone), saw the mouthpiece into its final shape with a coping or turning saw. The top is done, the foot now begun.

Foot

Proceed with the foot of the recorder just as you did with the flute. Start with a ⅜-inch auger and finish up with a ½-inch-diameter one. You can make a reamer similar to the one for the flute or adopt a more rough-and-ready method such as leveling the steps by stroking the inner walls with a long installers twisty bit. You will need hickory mandrels for turning the outside of the recorder foot. The tenon that joins the foot to the top is particularly fragile. Be sure that the mandrel is not so tight a fit that it splits the end of the tenon. To ensure a snug fit into the socket of the top piece, turn the tenon just a bit undersized and wrap it with thread. Rub the thread with cork grease from an instrument shop, which, with luck, might also carry the proper lapping thread for the wrapping.

Lay out and drill the fingerholes according to the table. These can be further tuned by enlarging a hole to raise its pitch. You can play the recorder now, but for any real use it needs a moisture-proof finish.

[opposite]
The red cedar fipple plug has a thin, flat slat glued to one side to fit into the chiseled windway. When all is well, use a coping saw to cut away the mouthpiece.

Turning the tenon on the foot to fit the socket in the top piece is a critical step. The mandrel at center fits into both pieces and can be used as a guide for the finished diameter of the tenon. Notice the shoulder within the socket that makes the bore smooth throughout the whole length of the instrument.

Joseph Moxon also gave advice on finishing boxwood. "Lastly, . . . hold either a piece of Seal-skin or *Dutch* Reeds (whose outer Skin or Filme somewhat finely cuts) pretty hard against the Work, and so make it smooth enough to polish . . . with *Bees-wax*, viz. by holding *Bees-wax* against it, till it have sufficiently toucht it all over; and press it hard into it by holding hard the edge of a Flat piece of hard Wood, . . . as the Work is going about . . . set a Gloss on it with a very dry Woollen Rag, lightly smear'd with *Sallad Oyl*."

The Dutch reed, scouring rush, or horsetail plant mentioned by Moxon is the genus Equisetum. *It has abrasive silica in all parts of the plant and will put a fine polish on wood and metal. This is an ancient fernlike plant that once grew as trees. There is a patch growing where Quarterpath Road crosses the dam at Tutter's Pond on the east side of Williamsburg, Virginia (should you be in the neighborhood).*

Joseph Moxon, the patron of how-to writers in the English language.

THREE CENTURIES OF WOODWORKING WITH JOSEPH MOXON

Joseph Moxon taught us so many things that I shall end this collection with Moxon's beginning. On the flyleaf of his *Mechanick Exercises* were the words: "Began Jan. 1. 1677. And intended to be Monthly continued."

And suddenly the secrets of the woodworker were revealed to all who could read. Joseph Moxon's *Mechanick Exercises* was not only the first real how-to book, it was also the first book to be published in monthly installments. All who enjoy reading and writing about woodworking owe an eternal debt to Joseph Moxon. His influence lies like DNA at the heart of all how-to writing. Moxon's 300-page book has been copied and rewritten for centuries, but, like Shakespeare and home cooking, nothing beats the original. He is the wood-writer's colorful and insightful ancestor, and his work is worth getting to know.

Moxon began his book with a discourse on blacksmithing, reasoning that woodworkers depended on the smiths for their tools. He then started off the woodworking section by examining the tools, telling how to "use them with more ease and delight, and make both quicker and nearer Work with them." The woodworker of Moxon's day could buy a wide variety of sophisticated hand- and foot-powered tools, but, as ever, the buyer had to exercise caution. Many of the handsaws of that time were made from hammer-hardened iron rather than from fine rolled steel. The hammering and grinding produced saws of uneven quality, and Moxon instructed his readers how to avoid getting stuck with a bad one. Moxon was writing in 1678, but watch anyone shopping for saws at the hardware store today, and sooner or later you will see people performing Moxon's final test. They will flex the saw in their hands, as have millions before them, knowing that "if it bend into a regular bow all the way, and be stiff, the Blade is good."

No woodworking book or magazine would be complete without its share of shop tricks. When Moxon gets around to discussing hammers, he digresses onto a trick that, . . . well, you be the judge.

A little trick that is sometimes used among some (that would be thought cunning Carpenters) is privately to touch the Head of the Nail with a little Ear-wax, and then lay a Wager with a stranger to the Trick that he shall not drive that Nail up to the Head with so many blows. The stranger thinks that he shall assuredly win, but does assuredly lose; for the Hammer no sooner touches the Head of the Nail, but instead of entering the Wood it flies away, notwithstanding his utmost care in striking it down-right.

Most of the book, though, contains solid instructions on basic technique. Moxon told his readers how to accurately dimension stock. He told them how to cut a mortice-and-tenon joint and how to offset the peg holes

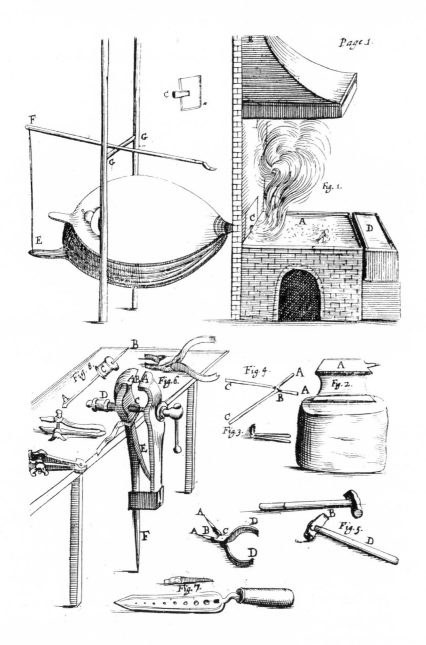

by "about the thickness of a Shilling" so that the joint would be drawn tighter as the peg was driven in. He told how to make an eight-sided picture frame and how to lay a tight floor. He covered basic woodturning, beginning with building a lathe.

Moxon knew then what still makes the home woodworker tick. He shamelessly advocated making things that have no purpose but to "make others that know not the way how it is done to Admire their Skill." One such feat was turning a freely moving ivory cube within an ivory sphere "with but one Hole on the outside to work at." He advised his readers to make the cube large and the hole in the sphere small "to make this Thing more Admirable to the ignorant Spectator, . . . that it may the more puzzle the Wit of the Enquirer."

Moxon began his Mechanick Exercises *with blacksmithing because all other trades "have dependance upon the Smith's Trade, and not the Smith upon them."*

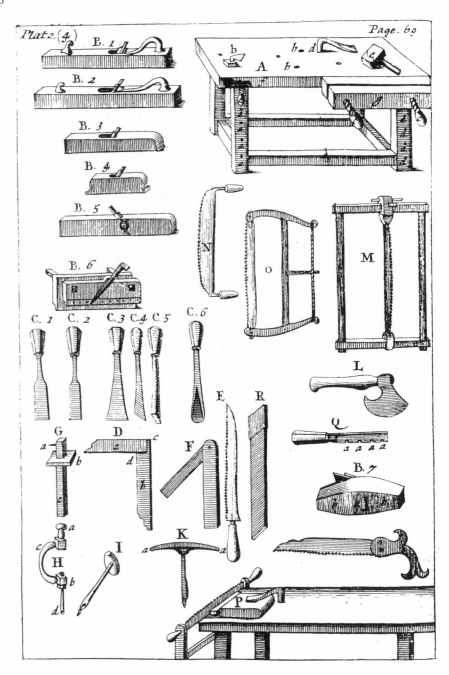

Much of Moxon's plate of joiners' tools was borrowed from an earlier French work, but considering the standards of the time he was remarkably original.

Despite his inclusion of such virtuoso projects in his writings, Moxon knew the limits of book learning. "This Craft of the Hand must be acquired with some continued Use and Practice, which will better inform your Judgement what Errors you may be subject to commit, than many words." Moxon's words live on, however, to this day and beyond. His text was appropriated by dozens of authors in the centuries after his death, and his ideas by hundreds more. Every woodworking book since has had some trace of Moxon in it. Woodcrafters will always know what Joseph Moxon knew three centuries ago: "How pleasant and healthey this their Diversion is."

Sources

Further Reading

Abbott, Mike. *Green Woodwork: Working with Wood the Natural Way*. London: Guild of Master Craftsman Production, Ltd., 1989.

Amman, Jost, and Hans Sachs. *The Book of Trades*. 1568. Reprint. New York: Dover Publications, Inc., 1973.

Arnold, James. *The Shell Book of Country Crafts*. London: John Baker Publishers, 1968.

Banek, Reinhold, and Jon Scoville. *Sound Designs: A Handbook of Musical Instrument Building*. Berkeley, Calif.: Ten Speed Press, 1980.

Bealer, Alex W. *The Art of Blacksmithing*. New York: Funk and Wagnalls, 1976.

Beard, D. C. *Shelters, Shacks, and Shanties*. New York: Charles Scribner's Sons, 1972.

Beirne, Rosamond, and John Scarff. *William Buckland: Architect of Virginia and Maryland*. Baltimore: Maryland Historical Society, 1958.

Bettesworth, A., and C. Hitch. *The Builder's Dictionary*. 2 vols. London: n.p., 1734.

Buchanan, George. *Making Stringed Instruments: A Workshop Guide*. New York: Sterling Publishing Co., 1990.

Butz, Richard. *How to Carve Wood*. Newtown, Conn.: Taunton Press, 1985.

Carson, Cary, et al. "Impermanent Architecture in the Southern American Colonies." *Winterthur Portfolio* 10, no. 2/3 (1981).

COSIRA. *The Blacksmith's Craft*. New York: Macmillan, 1987.

Croeber, Theodora. *Ishi, Last of His Tribe*. New York: Bantam Books, 1973.

Diderot, Denis, et al. *Encyclopédie*. 17 vols. Paris, 1751–65.

Dunbar, Michael. *Restoring, Tuning, and Using Classic Woodworking Tools*. New York: Sterling Publishing Co., 1989.

Eaton, Allen. *Handicrafts of the Southern Highlands*. New York: Russell Sage Foundation, 1937.

Fink, Daniel. *Barns of the Genesee Country, 1790–1915: Including an Account of Settlement and Changes in Agricultural Practices*. New York: James Brunner, 1987.

Goodman, W. L. *The History of Woodworking Tools*. London: G. Bell and Sons, 1964.

Hartley, Dorothy. *Lost Country Life*. New York: Pantheon, 1979.

Hasluck, Paul N. *The Handyman's Book*. Berkeley, Calif.: Ten Speed Press, 1987.

Hayward, Charles H. *Making Toys in Wood*. New York: Drake Publishers, 1974.

———. *Woodwork Joints*. New York: Sterling Publishing Co., 1979.

Hazen, Edward. *Popular Technology*. 2 vols. Albany, N.Y.: Early American Industries Association, 1981.

Hewitt, Cecil. *The Development of Carpentry, 1200–1700: An Essex Study*. Newton Abbot, Eng.: David and Charles, 1969.

Hindle, Brooke, ed. *America's Wooden Age*. Tarrytown, N.Y.: Sleepy Hollow Restorations, 1975.

———. *The Pursuit of Science in Revolutionary America, 1735–1789*. New York: W. W. Norton, 1956.

Holtzapffel, Charles. *Turning and Mechanical Manipulation*. 2 vols. London: Holtzapffel, 1875.

Holtzapffel, John Jacob. *Hand or Simple Turning: Principles and Practice*. New York: Dover, 1976.

Hulot, M. *L'art du tourneur mécanicien*. Paris: Roubo, 1775.

Hummel, Charles. *With Hammer in Hand*. Charlottesville: University Press of Virginia, 1968.

Jones, Bernard E., ed. *The Complete Woodworker*. Berkeley, Calif.: Ten Speed Press, 1980.

———. *The Practical Woodworker*. Berkeley, Calif.: Ten Speed Press, 1983.

Jones, Michael Owen. *The Hand Made

Object and Its Maker. Berkeley: University of California Press, 1975.

Jordan, Terry. *American Log Buildings: An Old World Heritage*. Chapel Hill: University of North Carolina Press, 1985.

Kettell, Russell Hawes. *The Pine Furniture of Early New England*. New York: Dover, 1956.

Klemm, Friedrich. *A History of Western Technology*. New York: Charles Scribner's Sons, 1959.

Knight, Edward H. *Knight's American Mechanical Dictionary*. 3 vols. Boston: Houghton, Osgood, and Co., 1880.

Mercer, Henry. *Ancient Carpenter's Tools*. Doylestown, Pa.: Bucks County Historical Society, 1929.

Mowat, W., and A. Mowat. *A Treatise on Stairbuilding and Handrailing*. Fresno, Calif.: Linden Publishing Co., 1985.

Moxon, Joseph. *Mechanick Exercises*. London: n.p., 1678.

Mussey, Barrows. *A Book of Country Things*. Brattleboro, Vt.: Stephen Greene Press, 1965.

Nicholson, Peter. *Mechanical Exercises*. London: n.p., 1678.

Noel-Hume, Ivor. *Martin's Hundred*. New York: Alfred A. Knopf, 1982.

Nutting, Wallace. *Furniture of the Pilgrim Century*. New York: Bonanza Books, 1921.

Pain, F. *The Practical Wood Turner*. London: Bell and Hyman, 1983.

Peterson, Charles E. *The Carpenter's Company of the City and County of Philadelphia 1786 Rule Book*. Princeton: Pyne Press, 1971.

Phelps, Hermann. *The Craft of Log Building*. 1942. Reprint. Ottawa, Ont.: Lee Valley Tools, 1982.

Plumier, Charles. *L'art du tourner*. Lyon: Jean Certe, 1701.

Pollack, Emil, and Martyl Pollack. *A Guide to American Wooden Planes and Their Makers*. Morristown, N.J.: Astragal Press, 1987.

Reed, Tim. *The Loom Book*. New York: Charles Scribner's Sons, 1973.

Rempel, John I. *Building with Wood and Other Aspects of Nineteenth-century Building in Central Canada*. Toronto: University of Toronto Press, 1976.

Richardson, T. *Practical Blacksmithing*. New York: Weathervane Books, 1978.

Ritchie, Jean. *Jean Ritchie's Dulcimer People*. New York: Oak Publications, n.d.

Roberts, Ken. *Wooden Planes in 19th Century America*. 3 vols. Fitzwilliam, N.H.: Ken Roberts Publishing Co., 1983.

Robinson, Trevor. *The Amateur Wind Instrument Maker*. Amherst: University of Massachusetts Press, 1973.

Roubo, André-Jacob. *L'art du menuisier*. Paris: n.p., 1769–75.

Salamon, R. A. *Dictionary of Tools Used in the Woodworking and Allied Trades, ca. 1700–1970*. New York: Charles Scribner's Sons, 1975.

Salivet, Louis Georges Isaac. *Manuel du tourneur*. Paris: Bergeron, 1816.

Schnacke, Dick. *American Fork Toys: How to Make Them*. New York: G. P. Putnam's Sons, 1985.

Seton, Ernest Thompson. *Two Little Savages*. New York: Doubleday Page and Co., 1903.

Smith, Joseph. *Explanation or Key to the Various Manufactories of Sheffield*. Sheffield, Eng.: n.p., 1816.

Stokes, Gordon. *Modern Wood Turning*. New York: Sterling Publishing Co., 1979.

Tangerman, E. J. *Whittling and Woodcarving*. New York: Dover, 1936.

Tatham, William. *An Historical and Practical Essay on the Culture and Commerce of Tobacco*. London: n.p., 1800.

Thoreau, Henry David. *Walden*. New York: Modern Library, 1950.

Viires, A. *Woodworking in Estonia*. Springfield, Va.: National Technical Information Service, 1969.

Wahlenberg, W. G. *Loblolly Pine: Its Use, Ecology, Regeneration, Protection, Growth, and Management*. Durham, N.C.: Duke University School of Forestry, 1960.

Weygers, Alexander G. *The Modern Blacksmith*. New York: Van Nostrand Reinhold Co., 1974.

Windsor, H. H. *The Boy Mechanic: 700 Things for Boys to Do*. Bradley, Ill.: Lindsay Publications, 1988.

Magazines and Organizations

The Chronicle of the Early American Industries Association
The publication of one of this country's largest organizations of traditional tool enthusiasts and collectors. The EAIA is also a terrific source of reprints of tool catalogs and books on traditional crafts. The magazine is included in your membership in the EAIA. For information, write to:
J. Watson, Treasurer
Post Office Box 2128
Empire State Plaza Station
Albany, NY 12220

The Gristmill
"Published by and for the members of the Mid-West Tool Collectors Association," this quarterly magazine consists of articles on tools, ads for tool dealers and auctions, and a helpful classified ad section. For membership information, contact:
Gristmill Editor
Post Office Box 1038
Carmel, IN 46032

The S.W.E.A.T. Rag
What can I say? Published by my buddy, Fred Bair. If you join, tell Fred I sent you so he won't be so mad at me for being perennially late with my dues. Write to:

Journal of the Society of Workers in Early Arts & Trades
606 Lake Lena Blvd.
Auburndale, FL 33823

[Joining up with any of the above three organizations will get you on the mailing list of lots of antique tool dealers and small reprint book presses. These are all reputable folks and interesting characters to boot.]

The American Woodworker
Rodale Press Inc.
33 East Minor St.
Emmaus, PA 18098

The Astragal Press, Inc. (books)
5 Cold Hill Rd.
Box 239
Mendham, NJ 07945-0239

The Colonial Williamsburg Historic Trades Annual
Written by people who make traditional work their livelihood. Write to:
Historic Trades
Margaret Hunter Workshop
The Colonial Williamsburg Foundation
Williamsburg, VA 23187

Fine Woodworking
The Taunton Press
Post Office Box 5506
Newtown, CT 06470
1-203-426-8171

Popular Woodworking
EGW Publishing Co.
Post Office Box 5986
Concord, CA 94520

Wooden Boat
Wooden Boat Publications Inc.
Post Office Box 956
Farmingdale, NY 11737
1-800-227-5782

WOOD Magazine
  Meredith Corp.
  Locust at 17th
  Des Moines, IA 50336

Woodshop News
  Soundings Publications Inc.
  35 Pratt St.
  Essex, CT 06426-1122

The Woodworker's Journal
  517 Litchfield Rd.
  Post Office Box 1139
  New Milford, CT 06776

Tools

The Fine Tool Shops, Inc.
170 West Rd.
Post Office Box 7091
Portsmouth, NH 03801
1-800-533-5305

Frog Tool Company, Ltd.
700 West Jackson Blvd.
Chicago, IL 60606
1-312-648-1270

Garrett Wade Company, Inc.
161 Avenue of the Americas
New York, NY 10013
1-800-221-2942

Kestrel Tool
Route 1, Box 1762
Lopez, WA 98261
1-206-468-2103
Kestrel is the source for traditional
(yet high-tech) Native American carving tools. I think they're great.

Lee Valley Tools
2680 Queensview Dr.
Ottawa, Ont. K2B 8J9
CANADA

R. Sorsky
Woodworking Bookseller
352 W. Bedford, #105
Fresno, Calif. 93711-6079
1-800-345-4447

Tools On Sale Division
Seven Corners Hardware, Inc.
216 West Seventh St.
St. Paul, MN 55102
1-800-328-0457
Call for their enormous free catalog
and you'll find good prices on the
hand tools they sell.

Woodcraft Supply
41 Atlantic Ave.
Post Office Box 4000
Woburn, MA 01888
1-800-225-1153

The Woodworker's Store
21801 Industrial Blvd.
Rogers, MN 55374-9514
1-612-428-2199

Index